non-freudian personality theories

GEIWITZ

BASIC CONCEPTS
IN PSYCHOLOGY
SERIES

BAUM

NON-FREUDIAN
PERSONALITY
THEORIES

BASIC CONCEPTS IN PSYCHOLOGY SERIES

Edward L. Walker, Editor

GENERAL

PSYCHOLOGY AS A NATURAL AND
SOCIAL SCIENCE   Edward L. Walker

TEACHING THE BEGINNING   Edward L. Walker and
COURSE IN PSYCHOLOGY   Wilbert J. McKeachie

A LABORATORY MANUAL FOR THE   Harlan L. Lane and
CONTROL AND ANALYSIS   Daryl J. Bem
OF BEHAVIOR

QUANTIFICATION IN PSYCHOLOGY   William L. Hays

BASIC STATISTICS   William L. Hays

PSYCHOLOGY: A NATURAL SCIENCE

NEUROPSYCHOLOGY: THE STUDY OF
BRAIN AND BEHAVIOR   Charles M. Butter

SENSORY PROCESSES   Mathew Alpern, Merle Lawrence,
and David Wolsk

PERCEPTION   Daniel J. Weintraub and
Edward L. Walker

HUMAN PERFORMANCE   Paul M. Fitts and
Michael I. Posner

CONDITIONING AND
INSTRUMENTAL LEARNING   Edward L. Walker

PSYCHOLOGY: A SOCIAL SCIENCE

MOTIVATION: A STUDY OF ACTION   David Birch and
Joseph Veroff

THE CONCEPT OF HUMAN
DEVELOPMENT   Elton B. McNeil

PSYCHODYNAMICS: THE SCIENCE OF
UNCONSCIOUS MENTAL FORCES   Gerald S. Blum

ASSESSMENT OF HUMAN
CHARACTERISTICS   E. Lowell Kelly

COGNITIVE PROCESSES   Melvin Manis

SOCIAL PSYCHOLOGY:
AN EXPERIMENTAL APPROACH   Robert B. Zajonc

NON-FREUDIAN PERSONALITY
THEORIES   P. James Geiwitz

BELIEFS, ATTITUDES, AND
HUMAN AFFAIRS   Daryl J. Bem

CLINICAL PSYCHOLOGY:
AN EMPIRICAL APPROACH   Erasmus L. Hoch

ABNORMAL PSYCHOLOGY   **James Neal Butcher**

NON-FREUDIAN
PERSONALITY
THEORIES

P. JAMES GEIWITZ

Stanford University

BROOKS/COLE PUBLISHING COMPANY
Belmont, California

A Division of Wadsworth Publishing Company, Inc.

4 5 6 7 8 9 10 — 74 73

L. C. Cat. Card No.: 79-90087

Printed in the United States of America

SERIES FOREWORD

Basic Concepts in Psychology was conceived as a series of brief paperback volumes constituting a beginning textbook in psychology. Several unique advantages arise from publishing individual chapters as separate volumes rather than under a single cover. Each book or chapter can be written by an author identified with the subject matter of the area. New chapters can be added, individual chapters can be revised independently, and, possibly, competitive chapters can be provided for controversial areas. Finally, to a degree, an instructor of the beginning course in psychology can choose a particular set of chapters to meet the needs of his students.

Probably the most important impetus for the series came from the fact that a suitable textbook did not exist for the beginning courses in psychology at the University of Michigan—Psychology 100 (Psychology as a Natural Science) and Psychology 101 (Psychology as a Social Science). In addition, no laboratory manual treated both the natural science and social science problems encountered in the first laboratory course, Psychology 110.

For practical rather than ideological reasons most of the original complement of authors came from the staff of the University of Michigan. As the series has developed, authors have been selected from other institutions in an effort to assure national representation and a broad perspective in contemporary psychology.

Each author in the Basic Concepts in Psychology Series has considerable freedom. He has been charged to devote approximately half of his resources to elementary concepts and half to topics of special interest and emphasis. In this way, each volume will reflect the personality and viewpoint of the author while presenting the subject matter usually found in a chapter of an elementary textbook.

INTRODUCTION

This book is designed for all those people who do not desire a major treatment of personality theories but who need a brief description of the essential ideas of the more prominent theories. Also, some of us in some of our courses wish to use an approach to personality other than the survey approach: we prefer an "issue approach"; we want to spend most of our time on one theory (perhaps our own). Our most prominent emphasis is not on personality theory but rather on developmental, clinical, or social psychology; we are teaching education, history, political science, or communications courses. We may want a brief introduction to personality theories as a part of an introductory course. The need expressed here suggests a brief, inexpensive treatment of personality theories, a supplementary or "one-of-many" kind of textbook. This is the need I have attempted to fill.

Additional comments on the nature of this book are contained in the prologue. My remaining task here is to thank all those people who have helped with the manuscript in various stages.* G. S. Blum read the original and revised manuscripts and was a constant source of encouragement and constructive criticism, even if he is a poor golfer. G. P. Ginsburg, E. L. Walker, and B. R. Fretz also read the entire manuscript; all were helpful, especially Ginsburg's dog, which chewed up one of my worst chapters. Individual chapters were read by J. Atkinson, A. Bandura, W. T. Norman, M. Carlsmith, and J. Freedman; their help was indispensable. None of them can play golf well either, except Carlsmith. But he cheats. Uses a five-iron off the tee. M. H. Bond read several chapters and made several good suggestions, one of which was to lower my left shoulder.

Finally, the greatest impediment to persistence on a task such as this—namely depression—was overcome by the continuing efforts of my 2-year-old son, Charley. His capacity to enjoy life was a constant model, without which this book would never have been finished. I dedicate this small book to a yet small person—Charley—but not because he gave me joy. Because, believe it or not, he is the best golfer of us all!

P. J. G.

* Sandra Fisher, Nancy Kerr, Darlene Lapham, and Dorothy Hollenbeck had the unsung jobs of clerical preparation.

CONTENTS

PROLOGUE

This is a book with a very limited purpose. It hopes to formulate certain basic propositions about personality theories in general, describe in very brief form the essential ideas of a dozen major theories, and look at some trends and recent developments. It will not criticize the theories nor present the research generated by the theories, except to illuminate an idea or concept. Developmental aspects of the theories will be de-emphasized, as will clinical and psychopathological aspects. In short, it is a small book about what a number of psychologists say about the normal behavior of adults.

Theory and research in personality will be called *personology*, after Murray (see Chapter 4). Personology, the study of the person, implies a concern with the individual, and some have defined it as the study of individual differences. It may be too narrow, however, to speak of a concern with the individual. Such a definition probably comes from the traditional source of personality concepts—the clinical setting, in which one man (the therapist) attempts to understand one other man (the patient or client). In nonclinical research, the goal is more often the formulation of a theory which can be applied to an individual but is about the behavior of the *average individual*.

Personology seeks to predict and control the behavior of people. It is not distinct from other branches of psychology involving the study of perception, learning, memory, and so forth because all these processes are reflected in a person's behavior. A personologist is concerned with *all* the behavior of a person, not with some limited aspect of it. Thus the definition of personology as *the formulation of general behavior theories* is apt. The focus of personology is on *human* behavior, whereas psychology includes legitimate interests in animal processes.

Personality theories are almost invariably phrased in more general terms than theories in more specialized areas. The theoretical constructs may be more general in the sense that they refer to more stimuli or responses (the concept of self, for example) or in the sense that they take generally applicable concepts (such as reinforcement) from other areas without considering some of the fine details. Hopefully, in the realization of our dream of a single integrated and complete theory these fine details will be useful; but at present even gross notions that "work" are notable for their ability to excite personologists.

Before proceeding further, we should look at a few assumptions about theories and their components. While there is considerable controversy in philosophy and psychology over the best approach to theory construction, personologists usually subscribe to the process description given by Cronbach and Meehl (1955). Briefly, a theory is a set of theoretical constructs which are not observable, a set of observable events such as behaviors, and a set of statements ·about relationships between constructs and observables, between constructs and other constructs, and between observables and other observables. Figure 1 gives an example.

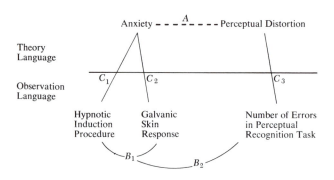

Figure 1

Aspects of a theory.

Anxiety and perceptual distortion are theoretical constructs which might exist in a relationship such as: "anxiety produces perceptual distortion" (line *A*). To test this hypothesis the experimenter induces anxiety by hypnotizing his subjects and creating a situation in which they feel anxious. The hypnotic induction procedure is observable and is *presumed* to induce anxiety (line C_1). To check on the induction, the experimenter records the galvanic skin response (GSR), which should be present if anxiety is present (line C_2). Perceptual distortion is indicated, in similar fashion, by errors in a perception task (line C_3). The test of the theoretical relationship, then, is given by the *observed* relationships (line B_2 in particular). If the *C* relationships are sound (valid), then relationship B_2 will test relationship *A*. Unfortunately the *C* relationships are the most difficult to state clearly, especially with the general constructs dealt with in personology. For example, if relationship B_2 cannot be demonstrated, one cannot be sure whether the C relationships are at fault or the A relationship.

The C relationships "cross the line" from the theory language to the observation language. When trying to formulate an observable related to a construct, scientists sometimes use the term *operational definition,* meaning the construct is so defined for a particular experiment. *Operational criterion* (or *observable indicator*) is perhaps a better term since the usual sense of the word "definition" does not apply here. When the C relationships are viewed from the other direction, from the observable to the theoretical construct, the term *inference* is used. When someone cries (observable behavior), you infer that he or she is sad (theoretical construct).

Now we can state another omission from this book, an omission made in the interests of brevity. The theories to be described will not be presented completely. The observable criteria for the theoretical constructs will be slighted, and only the theory-language parts will be presented. In some theories it is no easy task to find observable criteria; in others at least some will be noted, many times from experiments. It is to be hoped that this omission will be remedied by lectures or books of readings on experimental work.

We will be considering the theoretical constructs that various psychologists use to understand observable human behavior. We will see some differences and many similarities between constructs of these various theories. One prominent similarity will be detected in the functions performed by the different types of constructs found in these theories. For example, most theories have a "push" construct like "drive" or "need." Most have some kind of structural construct like "habit" or "trait" to indicate relatively enduring aspects of personality organization. And most have a "pull" construct such as "incentive" or "value." Whether all three types are necessary is open to debate, but usually all three are found—plus others, of course.

While most theories are similar or even identical in abstract organizational terms, the particular form taken by a given construct is by no means a matter of indifference. A "push" construct may be highly general and abstract in one theory but very specific in another. The name of a construct and its position in the network of constructs may be enough to cause researchers to study certain behaviors and not others.

In the next twelve chapters you will encounter the essential ideas (theory language) of a dozen important personologists. The principal criterion for inclusion of a theory in this book was that the theory be prominently represented in personality research journals. These theories, in other words, are the basis of much experimentation. Maslow's theory, which has yet to attain the research potential of other theories, was excluded. Atkinson's and Festinger's theories both failed to meet a secondary criterion of being general behavior theories, but they were so prominently represented in research journals that they have been included anyway. Since my emphasis is on approaches rather than particular theories, the factor-analytic theory of Eysenck was not included, whereas Cattell's similar approach was.

A special word in deference to Sigmund Freud and others working in his tradition: although Freud deserves inclusion by any criteria, his theory is so complex that an attempt to summarize it in a few pages would certainly result in severe distortions. Since several excellent summaries of Freud's and other psychoanalytic theories are already available in inexpensive form (for example, Blum, 1966), these theories have been excluded.

My intention is to present fairly and without criticism the essential concepts of the theories treated here. In such a brief treatment as this, an author may fall short of his goal, but perhaps enough of the concepts will "come through" to stimulate further reading or to form a basis for lectures by the instructor.

Finally, an apology is extended to all the thinkers and researchers whose contributions to a theory may even exceed those of the man by whose name the theory is identified. In science, perhaps more than any other discipline, labeling a theory with one person's name borders on criminal behavior. The only justification is that scientists are human and need some way to keep various ideas straight. The use of one man's name is a device to aid memory, and nothing more.

REFERENCES

Blum, G. S. *Psychodynamics: The science of unconscious mental forces.* Belmont, Calif.: Brooks/Cole, 1966.

Boring, E. G. *History, psychology, and science.* New York: Wiley, 1963.

Cronbach, L. J., & Meehl, P. E. Construct validity in psychological tests. *Psychological Bulletin,* 1955, **52**, 281–302.

In a field where concepts of man range from that of a collection of seething instinctual urges to an almost haphazard assortment of simple reflexes, Gordon Allport has tried to keep our attention focused on the object of our theories: man himself, with all his complexity, his uniqueness, his capacity for change. Allport's theory portrays normal man, conscious man, man acting as well as reacting. This creature, he asserts, must be understood both at the level of relatively isolated habits and at the level of life philosophy. To do this, Allport has formulated a theory that perhaps best exemplifies our definition of a personality theory as a theory that seeks to explain all the behavior of man. He covers all aspects, making many original contributions, unabashedly incorporating what he considers to be valuable insights from other theorists, and even raising philosophical questions that he admits are beyond the scope of psychology.

Allport has been called eclectic because of his tendency to use available ideas, from whatever source, when he deems them adequate. While this must be considered an admirable strategy, we will of necessity discuss only those conceptual contributions that are the essential Allport and that have defined his impact on personality theory and research. In particular, after a short discussion of Allport's notions of the Whole Man and his Individuality, we will examine in detail his major contributions to the study of human motivation: the theory of traits and the construct of functional autonomy. While we will thereby lose the breadth of scope that is so characteristic of Allport, we will retain what Allport himself considered "a theory that is concretely applicable to the infinitely varied forms of personal existence. . . ." (1937, p. ix).

THE WHOLE MAN

Personality is not an easy word to define, and Allport takes great pains to construct his definition. Devoting to this topic an entire chapter of his 1937 book, he reviews the many different notions included in previous attempts. Finally he decides that a truly adequate definition would be something like "what a man really is" (1937, p. 48). Such a definition does not make a commitment to a particular view of human nature (which, in Allport's mind, is undoubtedly a virtue), but it is also too vague to serve his purpose. Allport offers the following as an alternative:

Personality is the dynamic organization within the individual of those psychophysical systems that determine his unique adjustments to his environment (1937, p. 48).

The only term we need further amplify is "psychophysical." It is intended to convey the idea that human behavior and thought are the result of "some inextricable unity" of mind (psycho) and body (physical).

Obviously, this is a definition of the whole man, organized and dynamic. Everything that he is, thinks, or does is an indication of that unique organization that we call "him." Unlike theorists who pay lip service to this unity and then proceed to discuss or research only certain limited aspects of man, Allport has explored the implications of this grand view. Topics from heredity to philosophy all come under his gaze. At the important behavioral level, for example, he notes that all behavior has two aspects: coping (adaptive) and expressive. The former aspect is concerned with "what is done" and "why is it done"; expressive behavior is concerned with "how is it done," with the style rather than the content of the act. Most psychological research emphasizes the coping aspect of behavior, and Allport has made a real contribution by calling our attention to the expressive aspect. Facial expression, qualities of voice and speech, and stylistic components of posture, gesture, gait, and handwriting are among the topics explored by Allport in theory and in research (Allport and Vernon, 1933). There is theoretical significance in these notions for the psychology of the Whole Man because *what* he does and *how* he does it both testify to what he *is*. In 1937 Allport was willing to concede that the coping aspect gave the more important testimony, testimony which was to be confirmed or supported by evidence from the expressive aspect. In his 1961 revision the two appear on more nearly equal footing, a change foreshadowed in the 1937 volume:

The adaptive portion . . . is a more limited system, circumscribed by the purpose of the moment, closely dependent upon the stimulus and upon voluntary effort or upon habits of skill. . . . the *style of execution* is always guided directly and without interference by deep and lasting personal dispositions (1937, p. 466).

In this formulation, expressive behavior is said to indicate personal qualities not directly related to the immediate situation. You notice the gruff manner of a bank official when he asks, "What time is it?" This observation creates some anxiety as you contemplate that you must ask this same person for a loan in the near future—and then the harshness indicated by the expressive gruffness may turn up in the coping response ("No!") to your request.

The Whole Man indicates something about himself in everything he does. The Whole Man is also organized within himself; his various thoughts and acts are integrated and have a certain degree of consistency over time. This organization, at its highest level, is what we call personality. What is organized includes reflexes, habits, attitudes, values, and so forth. As a man develops from an infant to a child to an adolescent to an adult, one of the primary changes is in this organization, or integration, of his various behaviors. Allport considers five levels in this hierarchical organization, not all of which are present at all ages, at least not in the same degree. At the lowest level is the conditioned response, a simple act that, through learning, comes to be made to a particular stimulus. At a somewhat higher level, we may speak of habits—that is, integrated systems of conditioned responses. At a still higher level of organization, traits appear, which are (at least partly) integrated systems of specific habits. Also included at this level are attitudes, values, interests, and other constructs of this type. Traits eventually organize themselves into superordinate systems which Allport calls "selves." Thus, in this context, a person can have more than one self. For example, at school you may be suave, intellectual, and tolerant of other people's foibles; at home you might be unkempt, rebellious, and indignant of what you perceive to be your parents' hypocrisies. Finally, at the highest level we have "personality," the final integration of all lower systems, toward which we all strive but perhaps never quite reach.

The implications of Allport's ideas about organization can best be seen if we explore the notion of "self," here used in the sense of each person having only one. The constructs of self and ego are widely used in personality theory. After reviewing the various interpretations, Allport concludes that the term (self or ego) clearly means different things to different people, but the need for a construct at this level of organization is also clear. He therefore formulates such a construct and relabels it the *proprium* to avoid confusion with other interpretations. Proprium and its corresponding adjective, *propriate,* are related to the adjective *appropriate,* which means "to belong to in some peculiar or unique sense."

In his 1961 book Allport listed seven aspects of "selfhood" which are part of the construct of proprium: (1) bodily self: perhaps the first to develop, a sense of one's body and bodily sensations as peculiarly "mine"; (2) self-identity: the sense of continuity through time; (3) self-esteem: the sense of wanting to do things for oneself and take all of the credit; (4) self-extension: the sense that although other people and things are not within my body, they are still part of me—that is, they are mine; (5) self-image: how others view me; (6) self-as-rational-coper: recognition of a rational capacity for solving problems; and (7) propriate striving: long-range goals based on other aspects of the self— for example, occupational goals.

Allport feels that the first three aspects of the proprium begin to develop in the first three years of life and continually evolve until death. Self-extension and the self-image take form between the ages of four to six, approximately, and the self-as-rational-coper between six and twelve. Propriate striving, which depends on the development of the other aspects, generally appears during adolescence.

The various aspects of the proprium are all related to the *self as object*. They are parts of the "me," as contrasted with the "I," the self as knower. The latter aspect of selfhood is not included in the proprium; although Allport considers it an important aspect, he feels that discussion of self-as-knower takes us beyond psychology into philosophy.

As the proprium develops, it becomes itself a major determinant of later development. In this statement, we encounter another major contribution of Allport: learning can bring about changes in the very nature of subsequent learning. As he states it (1961):

Quasi-mechanical principles account for the emergence of the proprium; but once established, the proprium becomes the principle source of subsequent learning (p. 138).

By "quasi-mechanical principles" Allport means those typically associated with animal learning theories, such as reinforcement, repetition, and so forth. He feels that the application of such principles without qualification to humans overlooks the vitally important relationship of the learning task to the person who is to learn. Is he involved in the task? Is he "ego-involved?" These are questions, Allport says, that account for most of the variance in learning in all but the most infantile human. This is *propriate learning*. It is an attempt to understand the very common observation that it is extremely difficult to get someone to learn something he does not consider of value to *himself*.

A good example of the impact of this line of thought on modern psychological theories can be seen in its application to the quasi-mechanical principle called "the law of effect," which states that a person is likely to repeat an act for which he has been rewarded. Allport holds that, especially when the reward takes the form of success in an achievement task, the most likely result is not a repetition of the task but an attempt to achieve success in a task slightly more difficult. The person attempts to grow in competence and mastery. To blindly repeat the same act "is characteristic only of very young children, mental defectives, and compulsive neurotics" (1950, p. 170). This view of learning, motivation, and action based on individual interests and values has recently found a more complete exposition in Atkinson's theory of achievement motivation (see Chapter 12).

INDIVIDUALITY

The emphasis on the uniqueness, the individuality, of the person runs through all of Allport's writings. The first words in his 1937 book, written with obvious lament, are: "As a rule, science regards the individual as a mere bothersome accident" (p. vii). Science indeed attempts to formulate general constructs that can be applied to every individual; it is this method that Allport criticizes.

The issue led to the introduction of the terms *idiographic* and *nomothetic* into the general psychological language. Idiographic refers to the individual, while nomothetic refers to attempts to generalize. Allport sees theories of personality as having to do with the individual, whereas other branches of psychology properly seek the general dimensions, the general laws. Both are necessary, he asserts, but the thrust of American psychology has been largely nomothetic, even in personality theory and research.

How are we to deal with John, whom we now face and who is asking us for help with his problems? Will it help us to refer to our old psychology textbook? It might tell us that people who are highly anxious are susceptible to disruption. We give John a test called the Highly Anxious Scale, and he scores high. We tell him he is susceptible to disruption. John claims this is not so.

This situation is not an uncommon one for a psychologist or psychiatrist to be in. What is the problem? Or, better, what is the proper methodology for helping John, a unique individual? Using our questionable criterion, the Highly Anxious Scale, we have labeled him highly anxious. We know that there is a modest relationship between high anxiety and disruption. We accuse, but perhaps falsely. Maybe John fears social encounters because one of his eyebrows was burned off in a fire in his apartment last week. We search for a Social Anxiety Because of One Missing Eyebrow Test. None to be found; after all, how common is this misfortune? So, in desperation, we ask John, "What's the problem?" He says, "I'm afraid of going out in public with only one eyebrow. It embarrasses me."

This silly example illustrates in extreme form the plea that Allport makes to psychologists: if you are interested in the study of the individual, then study the individual, not the average individual.

By and large, psychologists have not accepted Allport's distinction between nomothetic and idiographic (Sanford, 1963). Even the extreme case presented, they point out, is nomothetic. Social anxiety is common, eyebrows are common, physical disability is common. What is uncommon (individual) is the simultaneous juxtaposition of the three common aspects, a unique configuration that is easily handled by nomothetic science (Holt, 1962). Truly individual, truly unique constructs are clearly impossible, both in science and in everyday communication; if they were truly unique, there would be no word in our language for them.

Recently Allport (1966), with notable reluctance, has suggested that he may admit defeat on this issue. Perhaps he should. But it would be to the great detriment of psychology if we did not recognize the tremendous impact of Allport's "rantings." He has taught us the necessity of assessing these unique, individual configurations and the danger of coming into an individual (or a group) assessment situation with a battery of tests based on *a priori* conceptions, fitting the person or persons to our own Procrustean bed.[1] He has taught us, in general, that personologists should go into an interaction with an individual with the goal of understanding that person, not of understanding some abstract theory.

HUMAN MOTIVATION

The problem of motivation is central to the psychological study of personality. Some writers insist that the two topics are identical. Although we need not accept this extreme view it is nonetheless true that any theory of personality pivots upon its analysis of the nature of motivation (Allport, 1961, p. 196).

Many psychologists treat motivation as one of several determinants of behavior, but Allport is one of a growing number of psychologists who take a much broader view of the topic. Motivation is seen as the study of *all* determinants of action, whether they function as movers or instigators or merely as directors of behavior. Habits, for example, are not treated as motivational in many learning theories, but in Allport's they are; they determine the direction of behavior once the organism is aroused. (See Birch & Veroff, *Motivation: A Study of Action,* 1966, in this series, for another example of this broader view.)

The determinants of action in Allport's theory are of many types: habits, attitudes, and traits, to name a few. His greatest contribution in this area has been the explication of the trait concept. Before we ex-

---

[1] Procrustes was a legendary robber who tied his victims upon an iron bed and either cut off their legs to make them fit the bed, or, if the victims were too short, stretched their bodies to make them fit.

amine this topic, however, we must first look at another major contribution to the study of human motivation: the concept of *functional autonomy*.

The concept of functional autonomy applies to motives in the adult human. It asserts that these motives are not related (in a functional sense) to the earlier experiences in which they originally appeared. For example, a child is born and raised on a farm. Later he moves to a large city where he becomes a successful businessman. Each summer, he spends his vacation on a farm. One might say that the farm has been associated with his childhood experiences of being fed, protected, and loved. But one cannot say he returns to the farm to be fed, protected, and loved (let us assume there are no relatives or friends on or near the farm at which he vacations). Food, protection, and presumably a loving family are now in the large city; still he yearns for the rural life. The basis for the motive, in other words, has been removed or displaced, yet the motive remains. What was, in a sense, a means to an end in childhood has become an end in itself.

Other examples of functional autonomy used by Allport include the ex-sailor who yearns to return to the sea, the miser who hoards his money while living in poverty, and the fascinating phenomenon of "craftsmanship," the desire to do a job *well*, even if the extra effort results in no material gain. The original reason for the behavior is missing, yet the behavior continues.

You may already have surmised that the concept of functional autonomy is still another criticism of prevailing learning-theory interpretations of adult motives. The attempt to take a few "basic" drives such as hunger, thirst, sex, and avoidance of pain and then show that all human motivation is directly or indirectly (derivative) related to these basic drives is obviously a task of great difficulty. Allport goes further: it is not only difficult, it is nonsense. A miser does not amass his pile of gold because he is hungry or because he is undersexed; he does it because he enjoys amassing gold. He may well have earned his first nickel in order to buy some food, but now the collection of money is an end in itself, related neither directly nor indirectly to the original motive.

Psychoanalytic methods which trace human motives back to childhood experiences are also being attacked here. In psychoanalytic terms, the miser might be thought to be suffering from the aftereffects of poor toilet training. Again, although there might have been some relationship at the time of toilet training, it does not exist now, at least in the functional sense. "The tie is historical, not functional," says Allport (1937, p. 194). We must be concerned with why he is doing it now, not why he did it then.

The reason we had to withhold discussion of Allport's notion of the personality trait until we explored the concept of functional autonomy should now be clear. Functional autonomy, as Allport states, "clears the way for a completely dynamic psychology of *traits, attitudes, interests,* and *sentiments,* which can now be regarded as the ultimate and true dispositions of the mature personality" (1937, p. 205). In other words, if we are to regard traits as the major determinants of behavior, we should not continually get involved with the time-consuming effort of tracing these determinants back to some infantile origin. If we do not regard our constructs as *basic,* then we should not use them as a *basis* for the understanding of human behavior.

As you might imagine, the notion of functional autonomy has had a history of controversy. Allport does not tell us much about the process by which the adult motive divests itself of functional ties with its earlier predecessor, and psychologists generally cannot bring themselves to believe that something happens unless they know *how* it happens. In addition, without knowing how it happens, there is no way of predicting which childhood experiences will produce autonomous adult motives. Why, in other words, doesn't everything you do as a child become a yearning when you become an adult? (See Bertocci, 1940.) Allport's reply to this criticism gives us a glimpse of a capability within his theory of systematizing the transition from dependent to autonomous motives:

Motives . . . may be autonomous in respect to their origins but never in respect to the ego (1950, p. 106).

The proprium, he is saying, once it is developed enough to take over further development, determines which motives are kept and which are not. Motives which increase your self-esteem, for example, will be kept. Motives which enhance your self-image will be kept. An example of this process, Allport notes, is the fact that there is generally a high correlation between one's abilities and one's interests. You may begin to play the piano under threat of punishment, but if you are quite good at it, soon you will find you really enjoy it.

Because of functional autonomy's relationship to the proprium, Allport in his 1961 book changed the label to *propriate functional autonomy.* He also expanded his discussion of process somewhat more systematically than our suggestions in the preceding paragraph and defined three principles that govern the incorporation of motives into the proprium. The first of these is the *principle of propriate learning.* This is essentially the point made before, namely that man's propriate organization determines what is to be retained (that which is congruent) and what is to be rejected (incongruent). This notion of striving for consistency is an important one in psychology generally, finding expression (more completely than in Allport) in Lecky's theory of self-consistency (Lecky, 1945) and Festinger's theory of cognitive dissonance (see Chapter 13), just to name two examples. It reflects a need felt by personality theorists for a construct defining a kind of psychological homeostasis. (Homeostasis is a striving for equilibrium, avoiding the disruption of an attained organization.)

Allport, of course, would not be content with a principle that dealt merely with the protection of past organizational gains. His Whole Man is active, striving to go beyond what he has already accomplished. Hence the second principle, the *principle of mastery and competence.* This principle states that whatever increases or enhances will be kept—that is, will become functionally autonomous.

The third principle is similar in emphasis; it is the *principle of organizing the energy level.* "There must be motives to consume one's available energies; and if existing motives do not suffice, new ones will develop" (1961, p. 251). Again, man is seen as active and striving.

In addition to propriate functional autonomy, Allport defines a simpler form which seems to be governed more directly by neurological and quasi-mechanical principles. He calls this form *perseverative functional autonomy,* by which he means a "mechanism set in action because of one motive . . . [continuing] at least for a time to 'feed' itself" (1961, p. 231). Examples are certain animal perseverative activity, addictions, and things done simply because they are familiar or traditional (routines).

While the question of how motives become autonomous could certainly stand more detailed explanation, the concept of functional autonomy has had a great impact on personality theories and research. As we noted previously, it is the foundation for the explanation of human behavior in terms of traits, one of the most widely used concepts in the field. It enables one to postulate, say, the "motive to achieve" as a determinant of behavior without requiring one to demonstrate that the motive is a truly basic (unlearned) drive. In general terms, the concept of functional autonomy frees "the theorist or investigator from unnecessary preoccupation with the history of the organism" (Hall and Lindzey, 1957, p. 259). It must be recognized that this latter impact would be of great value even if the concept were poorly formulated or complete nonsense. To predict the choice of a man walking into a sporting goods shop with money to spend usually requires no more than some information on his interests. (Does he prefer fishing or hunting?) To inquire beyond his present interests, to childhood experiences, would be a tremendous waste of time except when dealing with very disturbed individuals.

Let us now turn to Allport's theory of traits, which is perhaps his most important contribution. A trait, you will remember, is neither the highest nor the lowest level of organization in Allport's system. Selves and personality are superordinate, while habits and reflexes are subordinate. It is, Allport believes, the proper level at which to understand human behavior and thought, being neither too general nor too specific. A trait is defined as

. . . a generalized and focalized neuropsychic system (peculiar to the individual), with the capacity to render many stimuli functionally equivalent, and to initiate and guide consistent (equivalent) forms of adaptive and expressive behavior (1937, p. 295).

What we must further explain here is the notion of equivalence as applied to stimuli and responses. There is, first of all, a rejection of highly specific approaches that consider each stimulus and each response separately. The trait, as a mediator of stimulus and response, renders many stimuli equivalent in the sense that they all trigger the same response. On the response side, equivalence means that many different responses have essentially the same function in terms of the trait. Take, for example, the case of the (fictitious) Mr. McCarley (Allport, 1961) who has the trait we shall call "Communist-phobia." His trait renders equivalent the social stimuli of "Russians, most college professors, all liberals, all peace organizations, the United Nations itself, antisegregationists, and Jews" (p. 322). They all produce a hostile response, and this response may consist of writing hostile letters to newspapers, voting for right wing political candidates, throwing rocks at the objectionable stimulus person, or any one of a number of more or less *equivalent* responses.

A trait is clearly a theoretical construct, not something that we can directly observe. How then are we to determine the presence or absence of a trait? The general answer to this question can be simply stated: A trait is known by (or inferred from) consistencies in behavior and regularities in thought and action. In practice, identification of a trait is somewhat more difficult, but if you observe the person for a long enough period of time and in enough different situations, you will presumably observe that there are certain classes of stimuli within which he discriminates poorly, if at all, and that there are certain classes of his responses within which there seems to be a high degree of interchangeability. The person under study, who after all has a capacity for speech, may tell you directly that Russians, liberals, and civil rights organizations are "all a bunch of dirty Commies" and "we've got to do something about them." Like what, for instance? "Like speaking out against them, like voting for Senator Pure Andclean, like bombing their capital, like . . ."

Once you have surmised a certain class of equivalent stimuli and an associated class of equivalent responses, you infer a trait. Labeling that trait is a somewhat arbitrary matter and of little consequence as long as the label is not misleading—that is, does no injustice to the stimuli and responses which it has rendered equivalent. You may term a trait "self-pitying" or "martyr complex"; either is roughly equivalent to the other. Allport and Odbert (1936) have listed about 18,000 trait labels for you, in case you cannot come up with one that seems to fit.

Before we discuss the theoretical function of traits, we should note certain distinctions between kinds of traits in Allport's theory. The first is an artificial distinction based on the degree of generality of a trait (artificial because we are breaking up into discrete categories what is really a continuum). If a trait is extremely general, so general that there is scarcely an act or thought that is not influenced by it, Allport suggests we call it a *cardinal trait*. It is a kind of master sentiment or ruling passion. Not everyone, of course, will have traits as general as this. Allport cites the examples of Leo Tolstoy, who was said to have been endowed with a universal passion for the "simplification of life," and Albert Schweitzer, whose every act was said to have reflected his "reverence for life."

Less general but still highly characteristic of the individual are *central traits*. If you were asked to describe in terms of traits the essential characteristics of some person you knew well, how many traits would you name before you felt you had adequately described him? Allport (1958) asked this question of his students and found that 90 per cent of them used between three and ten traits, with an average of about seven. By this and other evidence he was led to suggest in his 1961 book that the number of central traits in the average individual is between five and ten. For example, a woman called Jenny has been analyzed (Allport, 1965) from letters she has written. She is, in terms of her central traits:

quarrelsome-suspicious	aggressive
self-centered (possessive)	sentimental
independent-autonomous	esthetic-artistic
self-pitying	cynical-morbid
dramatic-intense	

Do you feel you know Jenny? Do you think you could predict how she might behave in a given situation?

Finally, we have even less general traits called *secondary traits*. They are more limited and render fewer stimuli and responses equivalent; hence they are less characteristic of the individual. Presumably, too, the individual has a great many more of these than of the other types.

We should mention in passing that most of the time the following terms are considered traits by Allport (1963): attitude, generalized habit, sentiment, need, value, interest, motive, and so forth. At times he will make a distinction, if the occasion demands it—for example, if an attitude has an object of reference, is evaluative, and is somewhat more specific—but by and large all are seen as "inside tendencies," that is, traits.

Traits, in Allport's view, are determining tendencies or, equivalently, dispositions. Their function is, simply stated, to explain behavior. Traits can be said to underlie behavior, to cause behavior.

We are talking here about motivation in the broad sense in which Allport uses the term. Motivation is distinguished from other fields of psychology by its emphasis on the here-and-now (contemporary) determinants of an act that has just now occurred. Learning and development, by contrast, are fields of study that concern themselves with changes over time. What has been learned, of course, may be contemporary and hence motivational, but the study of learning is the study of process and change, the "how" of what is now present.

Motivation, for Allport, does not imply a "driving" quality that is contained in other theorists' conceptualizations. A person may have the trait "politeness," for example. We do not expect that person to run around exhibiting politeness, we expect rather that when he performs certain behaviors he will do it in a polite manner. Most expressive traits tend to be of this type. A trait, on the other hand, may indeed take on a "driving" character; that is, motivation does not necessarily imply drive, but it *may involve* drive. Perhaps aggressiveness is an example of the latter case. An aggressive person may run around exhibiting aggression, seeking every opportunity to do so.

Perhaps the best way to view Allport's traits is to see them as mediators between a stimulus and a response. The trait in these terms is dynamic, actively governing both the selection of the stimulus to which the person is to respond and the response made. A sociable person not only responds in a charming manner when in a group of people but also seeks out company when he is alone.

The trait by itself does not determine behavior. The situation that the person faces also plays a significant role, in many cases the dominant role. For instance, there are not many individual differences in church behavior. In other cases, the situation may determine which trait is salient. A person who "takes great pride in his work" and is also "verbal" may be expected to exhibit one trait in his workshop, the other when invited to speak to the PTA. It should be clear, however, that the individual is not a passive "reactor" to the situation; the situations in which we are likely to find him are often those in which he has actively ced himself. The most realistic way of stating this relationship might to say that the personal traits and the situation interact to produce navior. The two components are interdependent.

SUMMARY

Allport's theory is marked by his emphasis on the understanding the individual, and the identification of personality research with e study of individual differences has been heavily influenced by his proach. Although his discussions of "uniqueness" have often puzzled d even antagonized psychologists, his elaboration of the construct nique trait" has become an important theoretical basis for the exten- ve study of "common" traits. This strange twist of events is no doubt e to his insightful discussion of the nature and function of traits, gardless of whether designated as common or unique. The concept functional autonomy cleared the way for the ahistorical treatment behavior determinants; that is, it allowed scientists to formulate eoretical constructs about present personality and present situation ithout having to deal with difficult-to-substantiate referents to child- ood experiences.

The combination of (1) the focus on the individual and his present ersonality organization and (2) scientific constructs that "make sense" traits) has made Allport an important figure in personality research. Outside of Freud, Allport is probably the most important influence n the thought and work of clinical psychologists.

REFERENCES

Allport, G. W. *Personality: A psychological interpretation.* New York: Holt, 1937.

Allport, G. W. *The nature of personality.* Cambridge, Mass.: Addison-Wesley, 1950.

Allport, G. W. What units shall we employ? In G. Lindzey (Ed.), *Assessment of human motives.* New York: Holt, Rinehart and Winston, 1958.

Allport, G. W. *Pattern and growth in personality.* New York: Holt, Rinehart and Winston, 1961.

Allport, G. W. *Letters from Jenny.* New York: Harcourt, Brace & World, 1965.

Allport, G. W. Traits revisited. *American Psychologist,* 1966, **21**, 1–10.

Allport, G. W., & Odbert, H. S. Trait names: A psycho-lexical study. *Psych logical Monographs*, 1936, **47**, No. 211.

Allport, G. W., & Vernon, P. E. *Studies in expressive movement.* New Yor Macmillan, 1933.

Bertocci, P. A. Critique of Gordon W. Allport's theory of motivation. *Psych logical Review*, 1940, **47**, 501–532.

Hall, C. S., & Lindzey, G. *Theories of personality.* New York: Wiley, 195'

Holt, R. R. Individuality and generalization in the psychology of personalit *Journal of Personality*, 1962, **30**, 377–402.

Lecky, P. *Self-consistency, a theory of personality.* New York: Island Pres 1945.

Sanford, N. Personality: Its place in psychology. In S. Koch (Ed.), *Psycho ogy: A study of a science.* Vol. V. New York: McGraw-Hill, 1963.

The book you are now reading is testimony to the fact that there are no one theory of personality, but several. You may wonder why "someone doesn't sit down and take the "best" insights from each theory, together with the most reliable experimental data, and give us *one* theory that represents it all. Someone has, or at least has attempted to do so, and that someone is Gardner Murphy in his monumental work entitled *Personality* (1947).

The book in physical dimensions alone is monumental enough. Some 999 pages take us through the text, index, glossary, and the 749-item bibliography. The reader is nevertheless subjected to an apology in the foreword for several areas of research and ideas too "rich" to be included.

The author, Gardner Murphy, is well qualified to make the attempt. His frequency and range of publication have been almost unbelievable. One illustration: 1929, *Historical Introduction to Modern Psychology;* 1931, *Experimental Social Psychology* (with Lois B. Murphy); 1932, *Approaches to Personality* (with F. Jensen); and 1933, *General Psychology*. In five years, four highly respected and authoritative volumes, in four different fields of psychology!

Because of his explicit intent to take what he perceives to be the best ideas and the most reliable research from whatever source, Murphy's approach has been called eclectic. Murphy himself uses this term. In a new introduction to a reprint of his 1947 book, Murphy notes that the book

. . . is likely to be called "eclectic." The word means two very different things: (1) the juxtaposition of fragments from different systems, effecting a loose federation of essentially unrelated ideas; (2) the organization of a coherent theoretical system into which observations from different viewpoints can be integrated. It is in the second sense that I respect and try to accept this conception (1966, p. vii).

Eclecticism, however, is somewhat more. The eclectic begins with the assumption that each of the different views of personality has an element of truth but only an element; the theories are "partial glimpses of the truth" (1932, p. 354). Understanding this, the eclectic attempts to evaluate the different theories and "recast . . . [them] in a new unity," (1947, p. 12) with the implication that this new unity (or point of view) is destined to be recast by the next great eclectic in a kind of Hegelian timelessness.

Eclecticism is the hallmark of Murphy's theory of personality. Beyond this there is really very little that is distinctive about his theory, as one might expect. Our main concern will be the understanding of this "new unity" in which other views are "recast," an organization of ideas that Murphy calls a *biosocial approach*. While discussing the theory we will encounter several notions that, while credit is given to others, are more or less distinctly Murphy's; most notable among these are *canalization* and *autism*.

BASIC COMPONENTS OF PERSONALITY

PHYSIOLOGICAL DISPOSITIONS

In the prediction and understanding of human behavior, which is the goal of personality theory, Murphy broadly distinguishes basic components—physiological dispositions, canalizations, conditioned responses, and perceptual habits—from characteristics of the social environment in which the behavior occurs. Physiological dispositions are perhaps the most basic of the basic components. They represent the fundamental source of motivation and, hence, of action in the system.

It is not uncommon to see physiological and biological factors as underlying motivation—for example, tissue need underlying hunger, thirst, pain—but Murphy goes even further. He sees the basic biological sensitiveness or tension as more widely distributed, with few clear-cut distinctions such as are implied by terms like "hunger center." In fact, says Murphy, "every cell in the body is an initiator of motivation" (1947, p. 88). We can admit to degrees of motivation (tension gradients) but not to dichotomies.

This fundamental, biological motivation is active (not reactive) and continuous (it does not start or stop). All activity can be traced to its underlying physiological tension system, however complex that might be. More precisely: an instability or need in the biological system will have the effect of lowering the threshold for behaviors that are related to the need, innately or through learning or both. For example, hunger will lower the threshold for instrumental searching for food or, if food is present, for consummatory behavior (eating).

Since Murphy takes a broader view of physiological motivation, we can expect that he will concern himself with more than the usual "visceral drives," such as hunger, thirst, sex, and avoidance of pain. "Activity drives" are one additional class. Simple muscle tonus is a drive in this sense; it lowers the threshold for a response involving these muscles. More generally, Murphy discusses the general activity level of an individual, illustrated by the more or less spontaneous wriggling, kicking, running, and nonspecific moving of the infant. "Sensory drives" are a third class. Curiosity, manipulative behavior, exploratory behavior, and the desire for sensory stimulation fall into this category. Finally, since all the above classes deal with biological systems that are in a "state of readiness," prepared to interact with the environment to produce behavior, Murphy adds a general "wastebasket" category of "emergency responses" to handle behavior that occurs in unexpected situations (unexpected in either the cognitive or the biological sense). Stumbling over a chair in the dark is an example.

If we are concerned with some characteristic of an individual that will help us predict his behavior, we can attempt to measure some aspect of this biological component of personality. These individual measures Murphy (1947) calls *organic traits*, which are physiological dispositions on the individual level, the person's "physiological strengths and weaknesses, especially the strength of his drives; his tendencies to excitement and relaxation; his proneness to one rather than another type of physiological integration" (p. 130). We may be able to obtain a reasonable measure of a person's general activity level, for example. Numerous studies in developmental psychology have shown this dimension to exhibit rather consistent individual differences in infants that remain as the child grows older. Various psychophysiological measures, such as heart rate variability and skin resistance (GSR), are also of use.

In preparation for the discussion to follow, we must again remind ourselves that while these physiological dispositions are seen to underlie behavior, they do not determine behavior by themselves. Not only must the situation be taken into account, but also the fact that the primitive biological response and even the drive itself becomes socialized. However basic and biological the sex drive and its appropriate consummatory behaviors, the time of activation and manner of response in the adult human have become highly socialized; cognitive factors play a large role. Thus, even when discussing fundamental biological dispositions, we must recall Murphy's term: *biosocial*. Although we distinguish between biological and social components for purposes of exposition, there are in reality no pure examples of either.

CANALIZATIONS

How are the basic drives to be satisfied? Obviously through behavior, as eating behavior satisfies the hunger drive; but what *specific* eating behavior will be exhibited? Will Jim Doyle, when hungry, eat steak or hamburger? Will Ron Caple, when bored, go to the ballet or turn on the television set? How do we come to want what we want? Murphy here is focusing on a phenomenon of human behavior that has usually been slighted in personality theories: "acquired tastes." The phenomenon is called *canalization*. The term is equivalent to "channeling," and if you can imagine a kind of psychological channel connecting a drive with an object which satisfies that drive, you will have the essential image. More specifically, canalization is the "connection of a need with a specific way of satisfying that need" (1958, p. 64). "The energies awaiting an outlet break through the barrier at a given spot, are channeled or canalized in the process, and, as the barrier weakens, tend more and more to focus their pressure upon it" (1947, p. 162). A third quotation from Murphy provides the omnipresent biosocial emphasis: The "raw material of primitive human needs has been socially molded in a specific way" (1958, p. 62). Canalization is a theoretical construct designed to account for tastes, values, and preferences. If presented a choice between a baseball game and an opera, other factors being equal, we will discover the channel between our sensory drives and their preferred satisfier.

While their intended function is clear, we must be concerned with the development of canalizations. How do they come about?

Canalization is a form of learning, according to Murphy, that produces results with some peculiar properties. Contrast, for example, canalization with a similar learning construct, *conditioning*. Both develop in association with a drive being satisfied; both determine behavior once they are active. In the course of development, both follow the laws of learning—that is, the strength of each is a function of the number of repetitions in conjunction with a satisfying state of affairs, and so forth. Their differences include minor characteristics, but the predominant difference is this: Conditioned responses are subject to extinction, while canalized responses are not. Canalized responses are consummatory responses; they are, in a sense, their own reward. Since extinction refers to the procedure of no longer rewarding the person for his response, it makes little sense to talk of extinction of a consummatory response. For all practical purposes, one cannot remove the eating response *considered as reward* from the eating response *considered as canalized response.*

Conditioning is quite a different matter. The traditional Pavlovian example is the visual presentation of food to a hungry dog. The so-called unconditioned response is salivation (an instrumental response that facilitates satisfaction through eating). If a neutral stimulus, such as a bell or light, is repeatedly paired with the food stimulus, we soon begin to see the salivation response made to the bell or light even when the food stimulus is not present. The response is now "conditioned" to the originally neutral stimulus; when made in the presence of light or bell alone, it is called a "conditioned response." If you were prone to expansive description, you might say the light or bell has become a symbol for the food. Whatever your interpretation, you could easily extinguish this response by repeatedly presenting the bell or light without food. Soon salivation would no longer appear in response to these stimuli.

In Murphy's terms, Pavlov's dogs would have canalized upon the particular brand of food used in his laboratory, even as the lights and the bells came and went. The basic distinction is that the hungry dog can eat the food and be satisfied. He cannot eat a light, and even if he ate the bell, it would hardly alleviate his hunger. Thus canalized responses (acquired tastes), once formed, are with us throughout life. They compose a major source of the continuity of personality in that they are strikingly similar, if not identical, across the various temporal stages of life.

This is not to say that a person's preferred form of satisfying a particular drive will not change. New canalized responses are continually being developed. They may supersede older forms in the sense that they contain the essential elements or the same elements in greater complexity. The builder of model planes may become a pilot. A new canalized response may dominate a more primitive one. To love steak does not mean an earlier liking for hamburger has been extinguished.

It is worth noting that many of our biological motives are satisfied by things that we do with or to our own body. This body-canalization is seen by Murphy as basic to such notions as identity and the development of the self. Self-love and self-esteem are a kind of channeling upon a more abstract notion (self). Preference for one's own manner of intellectual analysis and the desire to "do things by myself" are just two derivatives of self-canalization. We cannot go into great detail about the many relationships and ramifications in personality that depend on the construct of canalization, but it should be clear that it is a powerful influence in many areas of concern to the personality theorist.

CONDITIONED RESPONSES

We have already defined the conditioned response. Although simple in schematic representation, conditioning reflects itself through the life of the individual so as to be of major importance. Organic traits, through conditioning, become *symbolic traits:* the light (symbol) represents food, and a person's response to the conditioned stimulus (light) becomes informative of biological disposition just as his response to food is informative. Language, a system of symbols, derives from conditioning. Attitudes are conditioned responses. Early conditioning—for example, early attitudes—may determine later conditioning. The construct of the conditioned response, therefore, is of great importance. But Murphy's contribution iñ this area is slight.

PERCEPTUAL HABITS

Perceptual habits are deeply ingrained ways of perceiving and interpreting what we see, hear,´taste, feel, and so forth. They represent a kind of integration of various canalizations and conditioned responses developed in the life history of an individual. Some of the basic issues involved in this integration appear in the concept of autism, next on our agenda.

AUTISM

Although the ideas are not uniquely Murphy's, his concept of *autism* is a major contribution, especially in the area of research. Autism is the interdependence of perception and needs; the major emphasis is on the influence of needs upon perception. In extreme form, a person may perceive what he wants to perceive or needs to perceive, even though "reality" is just the opposite. Freudian psychoanalysts speak of *denial*, for example, which may take the form of a person acting as if a loved one who has just died is still alive. In less neurotic terms, a political conservative may perceive the events in international relations as evidence that we must take a stronger stance against Communism while the political liberal simultaneously perceives the necessity of making realistic concessions. Obviously, perception is broadly defined, broadly enough to include general cognitive processes as well as "mere" perception. Thus, memory can be included, as illustrated by the quote from Nietzsche which Murphy uses to introduce his chapter on autism: "My memory says that I did it, my pride says that I could not have done it, and in the end, my memory yields" (1947, p. 362).

Autism, like all perceptual habits, derives from both canalization and conditioned responses. It represents a tendency to see both satisfying objects (related to canalized responses) and objects or events associated with past satisfactions (conditioning). As Murphy states,

one learns to perceive, think, or remember in this way because such a habit is satisfying, just as one learns to *behave* this way or that because such behavior is satisfying (1947, p. 365).

There are no new principles involved. The explication of basic principles, however, in the construct of autism has triggered a significant amount of research in personality. Before considering some of the studies, we must note a few corollaries of the basic proposition. First, it is Murphy's position that the meaning of autism should not be restricted to the distorted thought found in children and mental patients.

No percept or cognition escapes influence; autism is an everyday fact of life. Second, the influence of needs should be more pronounced (a matter of degree) when the stimulus is somewhat ambiguous. It is difficult to say it is not raining when one is getting soaked, but labeling a cloud formation as either an atomic bomb explosion *or* a tornado is an easier alternation.

These two assumptions are basic to many areas of research in personality. Festinger's theory of cognitive dissonance (see Chapter 13) applies most directly to *social* perceptions, rather than physical perceptions, because it is in the nature of social perceptions that they are more ambiguous. Projective personality tests, such as the Rorschach inkblot test, assume that their ambiguity will allow a more direct measurement of the individual's needs. The areas of research that utilize projective techniques for an indication of the elemental independent variables, such as achievement motivation, affiliation motivation, and power motivation, are in debt to Murphy's exposition of autism.

Murphy's own research includes some classic studies in the field of need-related perception. In one (Levine, Chein, and Murphy, 1942), pictures of various objects (food objects, household objects, and some meaningless drawings) were placed behind a ground-glass screen in order to create an ambiguous (not clearly perceptible) stimulus. Human subjects were asked to "verbalize an association" to each presentation. Need or motive was induced by having the subjects make their associations three, six, and nine hours after their last meal. The results show an increasing number of food-related associations as hunger increases, up to a point, after which the frequency of food-related responses began to drop. The interpretation is that the autistic process is responsible for the rise but that there is a simultaneous "reality" process working against autism and eventually causing a decrease in the food-related perceptions.

Two other experiments deal with the effect of reward and punishment on perception and relate to the proposition that a person learns perceptual habits by the same process that he learns behaviors—that is, because they are satisfying. Proshansky and Murphy (1942) rewarded subjects whenever they were looking at long lines or handling light weights and punished them (took away money) whenever they were looking at short lines or handling heavy weights. In a subsequent testing period, these subjects produced longer estimates of all lines and lighter estimates of all weights (compared to a control group without the previous experience), even though the rewards and punishments were no longer forthcoming. Schafer and Murphy (1943) used essentially the same procedure in a different situation. The final test phase consisted of an ambiguous drawing that could be seen either as a human profile looking to the right or as a different human profile looking to the left. Subjects tended to see that profile for which they had been rewarded in a previous session when the profiles were presented separately.

These experiments illustrate what Murphy had in mind by autism. The results and their interpretation have not escaped controversy, much of the criticism being directed toward the assumption that subjects were really "seeing" food objects, longer lines, and so forth. For a sample of this debate, which involves detailed discussion about the nature of perception beyond the scope of this book, see Pastore (1949) for criticism and Chein, Levine, Murphy, Proshansky, and Schafer (1951) for a reply.

SITUATIONALISM

We began with basic biological considerations and then turned to simple principles of learning. Taken together these processes were seen to result in quite complicated integrations that help us understand the high-level perceptual and cognitive behaviors of humans. Although there is an ever-present note about the biosocial nature of even the most primitive mechanisms, there is perhaps more "bio" than "social" in what we have so far encountered. We will now correct that imbalance with a more direct consideration of the social situation that a person faces when he acts.

Situationalism is the name Murphy gives to the approach to explaining behavior which asserts that "human beings respond as situations require them to respond" (1947, p. 867). This position is a respected one in sociology and social psychology; it assumes that, if your goal is to predict behavior, the most valuable information is given by the situation in which a person is placed and the social role that he is enacting. For example, if you were told that the situation is the presidential inauguration and that the role is that of Chief Justice of the Supreme Court, you could easily predict that the person would be holding a Bible and swearing in the newly elected President. Information on the toilet training of the Chief Justice would hardly improve your prediction. Most examples are less precise. But think for yourself of these common situations: a middle-class father speaking to a son who wants to drop out of high school; a Negro facing a white Southern sheriff; a man and a woman on their first date. Perhaps you cannot predict every event, every minute act, but certainly you could say something of predictive value.

How is the personality of an individual viewed in situationalism? Murphy states that it is viewed "as the locus of intersection of all the roles which he enacts" (1947, p. 866). No two people have exactly the same roles to play in life, and certainly no two people have the same situations to face. Hence, each individual is unique. But what is unique is not his biological system or his accumulation of habits, it is his unique position in society—a position that has provided him and nobody else with this unique set of roles.

FIELD THEORY

We have the "bio" and the "social" now. It remains to put them together into a truly biosocial approach. While situationalism has much to recommend it, the concept of the situation overlaps considerably with the concepts that apply to the individual. Take the social role of President of the United States. Clearly there is quite a bit one could predict simply from knowing the role. But who fills the role? Usually he will be an older man, above average in intelligence, above average in wealth. Generally he will have had considerable experience in dealing with conflict between people and between nations; he was probably a senator or a general before being elected President. The social role of President *recruits* a person with certain distinctive organic traits and with distinctive learning experiences. It does not make a great deal of sense to ask, "What difference does personality make in the role of President?" because one is asking for predictions over and above those that can be made on the basis of knowing the role. The role is correlated with the components on which we generally assess individual personality: organic traits and previous learning experiences. Hence, obviously, we can add little to the prediction.

The above example is not Murphy's, but it illustrates the finely tuned interdependence of situation and biological disposition that must be faced by the personality theorist. Murphy's resolution of this difficulty is *field theory,* a term taken from the physical sciences and, in psychology, from Kurt Lewin (see Chapter 10). Man and his environment constitute a field or system; behavior occurs in this field as a result of the dynamic interaction of forces within the field. Although boundaries are not clearly defined and are constantly shifting, there is one concentration of forces in this field that we call the person and another that we call the environment.

We cannot define the situation operationally except in reference to the specific organism which is involved; we cannot define the organism operationally, in such a way as to obtain predictive power for behavior, except in reference to the situation. Each serves to define the other; they are definable operationally while in the organism-situation field (1947, p. 891, italics deleted).

The basis for prediction, in this approach, is then the field, not the person alone and not the situation alone. On a simple level, this approach is useful in reminding us that the person selects those situations in which he wants to behave and selects, in a given situation, certain aspects to which to respond; the situation, on the other hand, selects (calls forth) certain physiological dispositions and habits from the person. There is an interdependence, which Murphy calls mutual selection.

The field, as a basis for prediction, enables us to get on with the important business of prediction without haggling about the precise source. If a social role predicts behavior, fine. What do we gain by arguing over whether it is in the person (through biology and previous learning) or in the situation? Behavior is neither "bio" nor "social," it is *biosocial.*

SUMMARY

The influence of Murphy's theory of personality is difficult to assess accurately. Certainly the continual attempt to integrate has supported similar attempts by other theorists. Borrowing from others, as we have seen, was also characteristic of Allport; the field theory approach remains strongly influential, especially in the more detailed form delineated by Lewin (see Chapter 10); and the integration of biological and social components into biosocial components of personality provided a needed emphasis. The discussion of perception as an aspect of personality, as exemplified by the autism construct, has been a major research influence; and the notion that "needs alter perception," although not uniquely Murphy's, is the foundation of projective tests. The Thematic Apperception Test of Murray (see Chapter 4) is an example of such tests; it is a device which has become a major research instrument (see Atkinson, Chapter 12) and diagnostic tool.

In his role as personology's reigning eclectic, Murphy has the task of sifting and evaluating available theory and research. It is a role not unlike that of a good art or theater critic, immensely useful and even more immensely difficult. That the attempt was made is notable enough, and the quality of the product is a tribute to Murphy's scholarship.

REFERENCES

Chein, I., Levine, R., Murphy, G., Proshansky, H., & Schafer, R. Need as a determinant of perception: A reply to Pastore. *Journal of Psychology,* 1951, **31**, 129–136.

Levine, R., Chein, I., & Murphy, G. The relation of the intensity of a need to the amount of perceptual distortion: A preliminary report. *Journal of Psychology,* 1942, **13**, 283–293.

Murphy, G. *Personality.* New York: Harper & Row, 1947. Reprinted with a new introduction, 1966.

Murphy, G. *Human potentialities.* New York: Basic Books, 1958.

Murphy, G., & Jensen, F. *Approaches to personality.* New York: Coward-McCann, 1932.

Pastore, N. Need as a determinant of perception. *Journal of Psychology,* 1949, **28**, 457–475.

Proshansky, H., & Murphy, G. The effects of reward and punishment on perception, *Journal of Psychology,* 1942, **13**, 295–305.

Schafer, R., & Murphy, G. The role of autism in a visual figure-ground relationship. *Journal of Experimental Psychology,* 1943, **32**, 335–343.

The "need for certainty . . . is very weak in me." In Henry Murray's self-report (1959, p. 49), we are introduced to two highly characteristic aspects of his work. The concept of *need* is perhaps his most important scientific contribution and it will be discussed later, but tolerance for uncertainty is a hallmark of what he is doing and how he does it. The study of personality, which Murray labels *personology*, is a science plagued by two demons: complexity and youth. It follows that an all-encompassing theory of personality is many years beyond us, to be preceded by many years of thought and research. We have to be satisfied meanwhile with partial theories and creative research that we can use as building material or "preparations for the scaffold of a comprehensive system," which is the title Murray gave his influential article in *Psychology: A Study of a Science* (1959). One does his best with what he has at hand and with what he can create. One tolerates uncertainty because there is no alternative; "you can't make a leaf grow by stretching it." (Hans Sachs, quoted by Murray, 1951b, p. 436.)

How does one prepare for the eventual comprehensive theory? Murray's answer is reflected in all of his writings. First, you take a good, hard look at your subject matter. Then you ask yourself: what is most characteristic of human personality—what *should* be explained? Then you apply good, hard thought to analyze that which is characteristic into basic components or constructs, trying to formulate these components in such a way as to be scientifically useful. The "scientifically useful" requirement obliges you to choose your terms carefully, define them explicitly, and specify exhaustively the means by which you infer their action within the individual (specification of operational criteria). Sometimes an additional step is necessary, the development of tests and procedures to indicate constructs that have no acceptable criteria available.

After noting certain general orientations, we will consider Murray's answer to the question of what should be explained and then proceed to discuss the explanatory constructs he has devised.

GENERAL ORIENTATIONS

We have already noted Murray's tolerance for uncertainty. It is well that he has such tolerance, for he sets as his goal the complete understanding of the whole person. His writings include both eloquent pleas for the viewing of personality in terms of complex integrations in the brain—"No brain, no personality." (1951a, p. 267)—and scholarly treatments of man in the context of his culture (Murray and Kluckhohn, 1948). He wants to know in what ways a man is "a. like all other men, b. like some other men, [and] c. like no other man" (Kluckhohn and Murray, 1948, p. 35). And he would have us be sensitive not only to the person in the present but also to the person in the past and the future.

Insistence upon the wholeness of the individual, of course, is a common orientation among personality theorists. Somehow, in spite of this, Murray's Whole Man seems Wholier than others. This impression is due undoubtedly in part to Murray's research, in which a limited number of subjects are studied over long periods of time by almost every conceivable method, from the most hardheaded of physiological measures to the most softheaded of interviews. Murray's *Explorations in Personality* (1938) describes the study setting and method in detail, and White's *Lives in Progress* (1966) is a fascinating modern example of this research orientation.

The study of *personality over time*—that is, the temporal dimension of man—forms the basis of Murray's definition of personality. The following three quotations are illustrative, with varying degrees of physiological emphasis:

1. [Personality is] the entire sequence of organized governmental processes in the brain from birth to death (Murray & Kluckhohn, 1948, p. 9).
2. The history of the organism *is* the organism (1938, p. 39).
3. Abstract biography *is* the personality, as far as it can be formulated (1938, p. 283).

WHAT SHOULD BE EXPLAINED?

Murray's definitions of personality supply a clue to his answer to the question: What should be explained? At the simplest level suitable for psychology, he suggests that we explain "organized brain activities." We could start at a more primitive level—for example, simple reflexes—but we are more interested in behaviors stemming from or controlled by higher cognitive processes in the brain. These higher, controlling activities Murray calls *regnant processes* (regnant means "reigning" or "ruling"). While regnant processes are seen to influence all human behavior, equal if not greater stress is placed on the temporal aspect of human personality. What is of interest is not so much what a man is doing per se, but rather what he is doing in the context of where and why and when he started doing the things that led up to the present, and where he hopes to "go." A student sitting in a barren room reading a book prompts us to ask, "What started him in a college education?" and "What does he hope to gain from this activity?"

PROCEEDINGS, SERIALS, AND EVENTS

Murray's basic unit of analysis is the *event*. An event is an interaction between two or more interdependent entities, occurring over time and resulting in some sort of change. The concept, taken from the philosopher Whitehead, can be applied to the smallest sub-atomic particles as well as to entire cultural systems. At a level of analysis appropriate to personology, we observe the interaction of a person with an object (which may be another person). An event at this level is called a *proceeding* by Murray. The person does something to the object or the object does something to him, there is an ensuing sequence of actions and reactions, and finally, for some reason, the sequence stops. Another proceeding begins. Most proceedings have a distinct beginning and end. For example, buying a pack of cigarettes may begin by walking to a drugstore, then asking, receiving, paying, and finally leaving. You eat lunch, study for an hour, then converse with friends (three proceedings).

Life, however, is more than a succession of simple proceedings. Humans think and anticipate. They set forth plans for their lives, and some of these plans encompass many years of effort. To set for yourself the goal of a college degree means that over a period of several years you plan to engage in a number of activities to further your progress toward that goal. You will engage in a number of proceedings related to that ultimate goal. For this aspect of human behavior, Murray uses the term *serial*, "a directionally organized intermittent succession of proceedings" (1951b, p. 439). The process of planning is called *ordination*. A preliminary phase consisting of imagining the possible consequences of various possible plans is called *prospection*. In addition to these three concepts, we could list several others explicitly labeled by Murray but could hardly do them justice with a sentence or two. However, the important point has already been made: Murray is quite concerned with explaining the long-term plans of human beings, and he feels we have neither adequate concepts nor adequate methods for dealing with these plans. Many psychologists would shy away from such a topic, without concepts and without method, but Murray has a tolerance for uncertainty for which we can be thankful.

EXPLANATORY CONSTRUCTS

Short episodes or interactions (proceedings) and longer integrated sets of intermittent episodes (serials) are the things (events) that Murray considers of maximum importance in the understanding of human behavior. The next step is to analyze events in terms of constructs that will enable us to recreate (synthesize) the behavior. Four major constructs will be discussed: need, cathexis, press, and thema. Finally, an emerging pair of constructs in Murray's system—vector and value—will be reviewed.

NEED

Murray's concept of need is his most pervasive contribution to personality theory and research. By his definition, a need is "a hypothetical process the occurrence of which is imagined in order to account for certain objective and subjective facts" (1938, p. 54). We would say, in our terms, that a need is a "theoretical construct" which is "inferred" in order to account for human behavior (objective facts) and thought (subjective facts). Murray later makes his definition more explicit:

A need is a construct . . . which stands for a force (the physico-chemical nature of which is unknown) in the brain region, a force which organizes perception, apperception, intellection, conation and action in such a way as to transform in a certain direction an existing, unsatisfying situation (1938, p. 124).

The source of a need can be internal bodily processes (viscerogenic needs such as hunger and thirst) or the situation confronting the person (psychogenic needs). Psychogenic needs stem from the situation both in the sense of that which is immediately facing the person and in the sense of the person's previous learning experience. The question of whether needs are innate or learned Murray does not consider worthy of much discussion. The point is to understand behavior by means, in part, of listing the motivating forces in the individual.

We must remember what Murray is trying to explain. An event (proceeding or serial) is a temporal construct; it has a beginning, then something happens, and an end state is reached which is presumably different from the beginning state (change has occurred). Need is the construct Murray uses to explain the beginning or initiating state. The end state is *intended* to be satisfying in terms of that need. That which "happens," the middle part of the proceeding, is behavior or thought related to the need and designed to bring about a satisfying end state.

Murray is cautious about inferring a need with any certainty. Several criteria (indications) should be present, for example, before it is assumed that the person is hungry. However, if we hear the person's stomach growl, see him look avidly at a picture of a juicy steak, hear him claim he wants to eat, see him take out a pan and cook something and eat it, then observe a satisfied smile, perhaps we would not be too far wrong in assuming that his proceeding was initiated by a need for food (hunger).

Needs are established more or less by inductive reasoning. One observes a person behaving and asks, "Why did he do this?" When answering, one must not be too specific. To watch the person eat a steak and then infer that he started with a need to eat steak is circular and nonpredictive. In many cases it is also wrong, as you could demonstrate by offering that person lamb or pork, which he would devour with as much satisfaction as he exhibited when eating beef. If, instead of a need for steak, you had inferred a need for food, you would not have been surprised to learn of the easy interchangeability of the various goal-objects in the class we call "food." Needs, then, are general in that they predispose behavior toward certain classes of objects or activities, not toward particular things.

Murray took a good hard look at the events in which his subjects were involved and decided that most of the proceedings and serials could be interpreted in terms of a rather limited set of needs. His list of common, manifest needs is a taxonomy that has found wide use in psychology:

n Abasement: Need to surrender.
n Achievement: Need to overcome obstacles.
n Affiliation: Need to form friendships and associations.
n Aggression: Need to assault or injure another.
n Autonomy: Need to resist influence or coercion.
n Counteraction: Need to proudly overcome defeat by restriving and retaliating.
n Deference: Need to admire and willingly follow a superior.
n Defendance: Need to defend oneself against blame or belittlement.
n Dominance: Need to influence or control others.
n Exhibition: Need to attract attention to oneself.
n Harmavoidance: Need to avoid physical pain.
n Infavoidance: Need to avoid failure, shame, humiliation, ridicule.
n Nurturance: Need to nourish, aid, or protect a helpless other.
n Order: Need to arrange, organize, put away objects.
n Play: Need to relax, amuse oneself, seek diversion and entertainment.
n Rejection: Need to snub, ignore, or exclude another.
n Sentience: Need to enjoy sensuous gratification, e.g., tactile sensations.
n Sex: Need to obtain genital excitement.
n Succorance: Need to seek aid, protection or sympathy.
n Understanding: Need to understand.

By now it should be clear that Murray frequently coins new terms and that he is prone to lists. Defining and listing (creating taxonomies) have often been said to be the preliminary phase of any new science; that is Murray's view, and he has labored diligently in that direction.

Murray has also distinguished between classes of needs. We have already discussed the distinction between viscerogenic and psychogenic. In addition, Murray distinguishes between manifest and latent needs: manifest needs are exhibited in behavior when aroused, while latent needs are inhibited. Needs can be diffuse or focal, depending on the degree of generality in the class to which they belong. Needs can be proactive or reactive. Proactive needs result in spontaneous behavior without regard to the environment. An example is hunger (n Food) which, when aroused, leads to a spontaneous search for food no matter what the environment. Reactive needs are tied to the environment—for example, n Harmavoidance, which is aroused by a threatening stimulus.

Needs usually result in behavior that is directed toward bringing about a degree of satisfaction. That satisfaction is seen on a qualitative scale of *hedones* (from hedonic, meaning pleasurable). The behaviors are called *actones,* a word Murray coined to replace "action" since the latter usually implies a need or an effect. Actones are pure motor behaviors (subclass: motones) or verbal behaviors (subclass: verbones).

The relationship between needs and other constructs is encompassed by the term *need integrate.* As needs occur, are satisfied, and abate, they become associated with certain emotional states, certain preferred goals and goal objects, certain preferred or learned action patterns, and so forth. A need plus its accompaniments is a *need integrate.* Hunger (n Food), for example, may involve the need integrate represented by the need itself plus its accompaniments: "pleasurable anticipation," a preference for steak, an abhorrence of horsemeat, a walk to the refrigerator, dinner table, or restaurant, and so forth.

Interrelationships between needs include *fusion* (a paid performer may simultaneously satisfy a need for acquisition and a need for exhibition) and *conflict* (a man wants to fly but fears bodily injury; he has a conflict between a need for achievement and a need to avoid harm). *Contrafactions* involve two opposite needs in sequence, as when aggression follows deference or vice versa. Needs vary in *prepotency,* their ability to dominate others when aroused; n Air, for example, is highly prepotent, for when oxygen is lacking, all efforts are quickly focused toward satisfaction of that need. Perhaps the most important of these terms of interrelationship is *subsidiation* in which one need is activated in the service of another. Murray (1938, p. 87) gives the following example:

A politician removes a spot from his suit (n Noxavoidance) because he does not wish to make a bad impression (n Infavoidance), and thus diminish his chances of winning the approval and friendship of Mr. X (n Affiliation) from whom he hopes to obtain some slanderous facts (n Cognizançe) relating to the private life of his political rival, Mr. Y, information which he plans to publish (n Exposition) in order to damage the reputation of Mr. Y (n Aggression) and thus assure his own election to office (n Achievement).

In this example, each need listed is subsidiary to the one following, and all are subsidiary to the need for achievement.

Murray does not ignore the problems of making explicit the means by which one can infer a need. Criteria are given in several writings (1938, 1951b), and the 1938 work is, in part, a giant catalog of needs and their criteria. One of the most famous of Murray's efforts in this area is the Thematic Apperception Test (TAT), a series of pictures of people engaging in various activities. Subjects are instructed to tell a story about the pictures, telling both what led up to the scene and what the outcome will be (note the temporal emphasis). Since this procedure requires the person to add much information not present in the pictures and also to organize that information in some coherent fashion, it is expected that the person will be telling you much about himself: his hopes, his plans, his way of organizing temporal existence, and, in particular, his needs. Needs and their diagnosis take up a major portion of Murray's works, a fact congruent with his statement about the function of personality, which, he says, is "to create a design for living which permits the periodic and harmonious appeasement of most of its needs as well as gradual progression toward distant goals" (Murray & Kluckhohn, 1948, p. 32).

CATHEXIS

Cathexis is a Freudian term which Murray has taken to indicate a relationship between a need and an object which will satisfy that need. The goal object is said to "have cathexis" in terms of the need, or we can say that the object "is cathected" by the need or by the person.

PRESS

Cathexis and press are very similar constructs in that both refer to the environment rather than the person. Cathexis is a term indicating that a certain goal object has "come into favor" in relationship to a need of the individual under study. Press, on the other hand, says something about the object or situation, independent of the person, that "pressures" a certain kind of response. Maltreatment by another, for example, creates a pressure for a person to respond aggressively; it can be described as an environmental situation with press for aggression (p Aggression). Press, therefore, is "a directional tendency in an object or situation" (1938, p. 118), just as need can be defined as a directional tendency in a person.

As with need, Murray makes several distinctions between types of press. The most important distinction is between *alpha press* and *beta press*. Alpha press refers to the situation that a person is *really* facing (objective observers agree) while *beta press* refers to the situation a person *thinks* he is facing (his subjective perception). Beta press is often the more influential determinant of a person's behavior, but both are important.

THEMA

"A thema is the dynamical structure of an event . . ." (1938, p. 123). It is composed of press and need—that is, the general nature of the environment and the general nature of the person as they combine to create a proceeding. For example, a person is rejected (p Rejection) and he responds with a need to reject that object that has rejected him (n Rejection). The combination of constructs (p Rejection → n Rejection) describes the determining features of the proceeding (event).

This was Murray's position in 1938. In later works, two developments led to a slight modification of his answer to the question: *How* is the event (proceeding, serial) to be explained? One of these is the development of the constructs of *vectors* and *values*, discussed below. The other is Murray's suggestion that in interpersonal proceedings it would be preferable to view press more in terms of the needs of the other person. We are to view two interacting persons as a *dyadic system*, a single system, "with equal analytic attention being devoted to each participant" (1959, p. 30). One person initiates the interaction (proceeding) because of his need or needs. The second responds on the basis of his need or needs. Murray is still willing to call the latter need-response a press from the point of view of the first individual, but only as long as doing so does not emphasize his needs over those of the other person in the dyad (pair).

Murray lists several dyadic thema which refer to the relationship between the needs of one person and the needs of the other in the dyad. By way of example, one such thema is complementation. Murray's illustration is a person with a need to inform paired with another with a need for information. We can assume that such a pair will usually transact a mutually agreeable proceeding.

It is also in this context that Murray seems to be moving from a traditional need (action disposition) theory to a more sophisticated description of personality in terms of *thematic dispositions.* Thematic dispositions take into account situations in which a person is likely to respond in a certain way. For example, instead of saying that John has a need for aggression, we would say that he is disposed to react aggressively to aggressive or insulting persons.

VECTORS AND VALUES

The constructs of *vectors* and *values,* already discussed in Murray's 1938 book, have become increasingly prominent in his later works. Vectors are action tendencies, modes of satisfaction (1938), or directions of transformation (1951b). Values are those "things" acted upon. Examples of vectors are rejection, bestowal, aggression, and avoidance. Examples of values are property, knowledge, beauty, and ideology. Events can be described in terms of a vector and a value for each participant in a proceeding. I reject a proposed loan. I *reject* (vector) *property* (value). I give my son a gift. I *bestow* (vector) *property* (value). I break a window intentionally—I *aggress* against *property.*

Vectors are ways of behaving toward something, and values are those things toward which the behavior is directed. Vectors and values are thus general *descriptive* terms, as compared to need, press, and cathexis, which are *theoretical* constructs. A thema (structure of an event) can be viewed on a theoretical level as a combination of needs and press, on a descriptive level as a combination of vectors and values. This seems to be the function in theory and research of vector-value terminology: a way of describing in somewhat general terms what happens in order to explain it in dynamic terms (needs, press).

SUMMARY

Murray's theory of personality holds that important human behaviors are related to one another in a temporal fashion (proceedings and serials). These temporal integrates are pushed (by needs) and pulled (by press), with the fundamental goal being the satisfaction of needs.

This skeleton outline of personality has been developed from the study of many individuals over long periods of time, over long periods of each subject's life. Sometimes the constructs seem effective but sometimes they seem to overlook strong determinants of behavior. (Note, in regard to relative ineffectiveness, the contrast between the early interpretation and later behavior in the case of Joseph Kidd, in White, 1966.)

In many respects, Murray's is a very typical personality theory; it is motivational (based on needs) with not-too-complex concepts to explain what may be complex behavior in terms of interaction between determinants. The development, within the theory, of thematic dispositions, dyadic systems, and vector-value constructs points out problems with the typical approach and is an insightful groping toward more effective treatments. "Thematic dispositions" imply a difficulty encountered in trying to identify motivation in either person or situation distinct from the other. "Dyadic systems" have a similar implication and, further, bring in a social or interpersonal emphasis that goes beyond the traditional intrapersonal diagnosis. And with these emerging, more complicated theoretical constructs, we find the simultaneous development of concepts like vector and value, which are quite descriptive in nature and much like summary classes or sets, classes of behaviors or objects. These concepts are not too specific, of course, but yet not too general.

Thus, from its original starting point, the theory seems to be moving toward more adequate descriptive constructs and more complex interactive theoretical constructs. The later constructs have a flavor of field theory, an approach we have already discussed in Murphy (Chapter 3) and will encounter again in Lewin (Chapter 10).

REFERENCES

Kluckhohn, C., & Murray, H. A. Personality formation: The determinants. In C. Kluckhohn & H. A. Murray (Eds.), *Personality in nature, society, and culture.* New York: Knopf, 1948.

Murray, H. A. *Explorations in personality.* New York: Oxford, 1938.

Murray, H. A. Some basic psychological assumptions and conceptions. *Dialectica,* 1951, **5,** 266–292. (a)

Murray, H. A. Toward a classification of interactions. In T. Parsons & E. A. Shils (Eds.), *Toward a general theory of action.* Cambridge, Mass.: Harvard Univ. Press, 1951. (b)

Murray, H. A. Preparations for the scaffold of a comprehensive system. In S. Koch (Ed.), *Psychology: a study of a science.* Vol. III. New York: McGraw-Hill, 1959.

Murray, H. A., & Kluckhohn, C. Outline of a conception of personality. In C. Kluckhohn & H. A. Murray (Eds.), *Personality in nature, society, and culture.* New York: Knopf, 1948.

White, R. W. *Lives in progress.* (2nd ed.) New York: Holt, Rinehart and Winston, 1966.

Sheldon does not have a complete personality theory in the sense in which we have defined theory, but the concepts he has introduced are so widely known that it is almost imperative to include them in a survey of the field. These concepts are not many, nor are they difficult to understand; indeed, the simplicity of the theory is perhaps its greatest virtue and its greatest vice. In overview, Sheldon identifies three dimensions of body-build, or *physique,* and relates them to three dimensions at the level of personality, or *temperament.* Both sets of dimensions are seen as measuring basic biological or constitutional differences between people. These variables come with convenient operational measures, making Sheldon's one of the few theories with constitutional variables that are of use to the average psychologist.

Let us now look at these constructs in more detail, first at the level of physique.

COMPONENTS OF PHYSIQUE

"Yond Cassius has a lean and hungry look; he thinks too much: such men are dangerous."

As the Shakespearean quotation illustrates, the tendency for man to classify his fellows on the basis of physique is not new. There are fat men, skinny men, muscular men, round men, square men, tall men, short men, all sizes and shapes. Sheldon set out to find a reasonable system for classifying these sizes and shapes, reasonable both (1) in that men could be put into one category or another and (2) in that the categories could be expected to have some use in medical and psychological theory. Men could be classified with great efficiency as "tall" or "short," but few beyond the basketball coach might find the categories of interest. The classification of men into "fat" or "skinny" offers more promise, since such categories seem to be related to certain medical conditions, such as heart disease, and have often been suggested as correlates of psychological traits—for example, fat men are jolly and thin men "think too much."

Sheldon's first insight was that classification into types in the crude sense would not suffice for any but the most extreme physiques. *Most people are average.* They are neither fat nor skinny, or—perhaps a better phrasing—they are both fat and skinny. In other words, we should look not for a *type* but for a *dimension* of physique—a dimension on which each person may be placed. I may have a lot of fatness, you a little, but both of us can be measured on the same dimension.

Taking a large set of photographs of men, Sheldon tried to arrange them along certain theoretically interesting dimensions and found, to his satisfaction, that all men could be measured on three dimensions. He called these dimensions *endomorphy, mesomorphy,* and *ectomorphy.* The terms come from embryology, from the three original embryonic layers that develop into the mature organism. The innermost layer, the endoderm, is most closely related to the digestive system, hence endomorphy refers to a dimension or component of physique indicated by soft roundness of the body, especially when the belly is large relative to other areas of the body. A man high in endomorphy would usually be called fat.

Bones and muscles come from the mesoderm, the second embryonic layer, hence mesomorphy is indicated by the relative prominence of bone and muscle. The figure of a person high in mesomorphy is usually hard, rectangular, and heavier than it appears: in our everyday terms, muscular.

The third and outermost layer of the embryo, the ectoderm, is most closely related to the skin, sense organs, and nervous system. Ecto-morphy thus refers to the following characteristics: delicateness of the body; great surface-to-mass ratio ("a lot of skin for his body"); and, presumably, a large brain relative to body mass. People high in ecto-morphy would be called "beanpoles."

As was mentioned previously, it is not proper to use these compo-nents of physique as types except perhaps in those rare cases in which a person is extremely high on one dimension and extremely low on the other two. Most people fall somewhere between the extremes on all three dimensions. Sheldon rates a physique on each dimension on a 7-point scale based on a number of measures. Each individual by this rating, gets a score such as 2 6 2; the numbers in the score refer to endomorphy, mesomorphy, and ectomorphy, respectively. Such a score is called a *somatotype.* The somatotype 2 6 2, for example, indicates a very muscular body, characteristic of top atheletes, not delicate and not fat. A 5 6 2, in comparison, has greater endomorphy along with the muscle and might be found among wrestlers. The most common somato-type among Sheldon's sample (1954) of 46,000 men is 4 4 3. The aver-age man has an average body.

Scoring the somatotype is not a difficult procedure, as the reader can verify in Sheldon's 1940 and 1954 treatises. The *Atlas of Men* (1954) contains 1,175 photographs of the 88 different male somatotypes identified up to that time. This atlas is Sheldon's attempt to present a standard file of good examples of each somatotype as an aid to objective scoring.

By now, while you may agree that people could be rated on these dimensions, you are probably wondering about the stability of the scores. Sheldon claims that somatotype reflects basic biological differences—that is, that the somatotype is innate. By this assumption, the somatotype must be stable throughout the life of the individual. What happens to a person high in endomorphy when, say, he gets sick and loses a lot of weight? Does he lose in endomorphy and gain in ectomorphy?

Sheldon has had to face these questions from critics who claim the somatotype is little more than nutrition, the feeding history of the individual. In 1940, Sheldon took a relatively strong stand, noting that certain determinants of physique do not vary with the amount of food consumed—the size and shape of the skeleton, for example. A fat ectomorph is not an endomorph. In 1954, after testing his categories across several age levels, he took a somewhat more conservative view. As men get older, they gain weight. Presumably the same distribution of somatotypes exists at age 20 as at age 50, but almost without exception the men are heavier at the later age. Hence Sheldon made the average weight history part of the somatotype:

More formally, the somatotype is defined as a trajectory or pathway along which the living organism is destined to travel under average conditions of nutrition and in the absence of grossly disturbing pathology (1954, p. 337).

The word "trajectory" refers to the curve of weights for the individual plotted at different ages. All somatotypes tend to become heavier, but some gain faster than others. To adequately characterize the somatotype, then, one should have the weight history. It will not only help categorization but will also lessen the chance of mistaken typing. If there is something unusual about the present weight measurement, whether due to nutritional abnormality (for example, starvation) or to "grossly disturbed pathology" such as glandular disease or lingering illness, the history of the person's weight should indicate it.

Sheldon is saying that the somatotype can be reasonably assessed under standard (not abnormal) conditions of health and nutrition. When one observes a person's physique, what one sees (the phenotype) is a function of nutrition, health, and the basic, or constitutional, physique. The constitutional physique (the genotype) can never be observed directly, but the researcher can make a reasonable estimate of it if he is careful to note the medical and weight records, thus lessening the effect on his judgment of fluctuations caused by the extraneous factors of nutrition and health.

SECONDARY COMPONENTS

In addition to the primary dimensions of physique (endomorphy, mesomorphy, and ectomorphy), Sheldon has identified a number of secondary dimensions. The most influential of these are *dysplasia*, *gynandromorphy* (the "g" component), and the *textural* ("t") *component*.

Dysplasia refers to a physique which is not consistent in somatotype. The overall somatotype is in every case a composite of regional somatotypes, assessed in five different areas of the body: (1) head and neck, (2) chest, (3) arms and hands, (4) abdomen, and (5) legs and feet. Dysplasia is a function of the degree to which these five assessments differ. For example, some men are slight and delicate above the waist but have very muscular legs. Sheldon suggests that a high degree of dysplasia is characteristic of mental patients, almost as if physical conflict led to mental conflict. On the other hand, the particular example given above has been termed "academic dysplasia" because Sheldon fancies "that men who are happy and successful in academic life often present such a dysplasia" (1954, p. 338).

Gynandromorphy is defined as the extent to which the physique exhibits characteristics of the opposite sex. In men, the body may have female features such as softness, roundness, and wide hips. Breasts often accumulate a fatty layer and sometimes are even functional.

The textural component is an aesthetic dimension. It refers to the *quality* of the body, to its symmetry and beauty of configuration, fineness of feature, and the like. There is a tinge of animal husbandry in this concept: "Men cannot forever ignore the problem of systematically gauging the quality of human stock" (1940, p. 75). It may come as no surprise, therefore, to learn that Sheldon grew up in a rural setting and that his father was an animal breeder (Hall and Lindzey, 1957).

COMPONENTS OF TEMPERAMENT

In a fashion similar to his analysis of body types, Sheldon attempted to develop components or dimensions of psychological temperament. Starting with a list of 650 personality traits, most of which were related to extraversion or introversion, Sheldon developed a reduced list of 50 which he felt contained all the ideas of the original 650. Persons were then rated on the 50 traits, and all 50 were correlated with one another. The pattern of intercorrelations suggested three clusters, which Sheldon took for his three basic components of temperament.

The first cluster, or component, is named *viscerotonia,* after the digestive viscera. The traits in the cluster include those with reference to relaxation and love of comfort, food, people, and affection. The second component, *somatotonia*, is named after the body (soma) and includes traits such as love of physical adventure and risk, competitive aggressiveness, and physical courage. *Cerebrotonia* (after cerebrum) includes love of privacy, mental overintensity, postural restraint, and social restraint.

Although neither the components of physique nor the components of temperament were intentionally developed to yield three levels, the above terms anticipate the relationship between constitution and temperament. Endomorphy correlates with viscerotonia, mesomorphy with somatotonia, and ectomorphy with cerebrotonia. This finding led Sheldon to suggest that true constitutional differences are involved at both levels, that they are expressed both in physique and in temperament. The fat person *is* jolly, the thin person *is* restrained, and the muscle man *is* liable to kick sand in the face of the ectomorph at the beach.

The correlations between body type and temperament found by Sheldon are very high, much higher than the correlations usually found in personality research. While one cannot dispute the statistics, the reader should be aware that many psychologists feel the reported correlations are higher than the "true" correlations. Their primary criticism is that the person rating the temperament of an individual may be influenced by the very same cultural stereotypes that are supposedly demonstrated. For example, someone high in endomorphy may be rated as more sociable than he is in fact; "everyone knows that fat men are jolly." Objective personality tests, not involving ratings, tend to show much lower correlations between temperament and physique, although some relationship usually remains.

SUMMARY

While the correlations of body type and temperament have produced much excitement and controversy among psychologists over the years, Sheldon would probably see his greatest achievement in the specification and measurement of physiques. He is most interested in underlying constitutional factors as they are revealed in body build. Once these factors are identified, even in a relatively crude manner, we can begin looking for personality, social, and medical correlates. Some of his later writings seem to say, "Maybe my temperament research wasn't the best, but I give you some readable dimensions of physique and some interesting secondary components. Perhaps these variables relate to cerebrotonia, measured by a better method, or to anxiety, juvenile delinquency, mental illness, or lung cancer. Why not find out?"

REFERENCES

Hall, C. S., & Lindzey, G. *Theories of personality.* New York: Wiley, 1957.

Sheldon, W. H. *The varieties of human physique.* New York: Harper, 1940.

Sheldon, W. H. *The varieties of temperament.* New York: Harper, 1942.

Sheldon, W. H. *Atlas of men.* New York: Harper, 1954.

RAYMOND B. CATTELL

6

Mathematics is a language that represents relationships between variables more precisely than does our everyday speech. All psychologists use mathematics, if only for statistical tests, but Cattell is known for his use of mathematics to formulate basic concepts in personality theory. We shall therefore have to concern ourselves with the *method* of inquiry in this chapter; the method and the theory are interrelated, each influencing the other.

THE METHOD

The logic of Cattell's approach to understanding human behavior is not unlike that of any other theorist. Every theorist seeks to conceive a relatively small number of theoretical constructs or factors in order to explain the tremendous complexity of personality. Although the final goal is the same, the approaches vary considerably and the resulting constructs often differ in form as well as content.

The constructs produced by Cattell's method, *factor analysis*, are dimensions in mathematical space which can be used to locate anything in that space. To understand what this means, we will use physical space as an analogy. In order to locate any city or town in the United States, you need two dimensions: "North-South" and "East-West." Every city is a certain distance north or south of you and a certain distance east or west. Additional dimensions, such as "Northeast-Southwest," are possible but unnecessary; two are sufficient. Factor analysis is a mathematical technique for identifying such dimensions, given certain information about the space involved. The final result of the analysis, "dimensions which locate," is not quite the same as the "constructs which explain" that are produced by other theories. For all practical purposes, however, we may consider them in the same manner, just as you might use North-South and East-West to "explain" your hometown.

The factor-analysis procedure for arriving at basic constructs is quite different from the procedures used in other theories. Most of the others use some combination of logic and intuition, usually unspecified, to conceive a construct and then test it for validity. Factor analysis produces the constructs (dimensions) for you. All you have to do is collect the things you want explained (located), find out how they are related (usually by correlations), and then send the results to the computer. The computer will return a set of dimensions necessary and sufficient to "explain" (locate) all the things you started with.

The mathematical space with which we are concerned can be called the personality space or, as Cattell terms it, the *personality sphere*. In one highly illustrative line of research, Cattell began by attempting to obtain a complete list of all possible human behaviors. He assumed that, if a behavior was important for our culture, it would have a name and would therefore be in the dictionary. Luckily for him, Allport and Odbert (1936) had already searched the dictionaries for all words that could be used to describe individuals. The total count was around 18,000. Many of these behavior-words, however, were not related to personality; they were descriptions of an activity rather than of a person (for example, "running"). By eliminating such words, by combining synonyms, and so forth, Cattell arrived at a much more manageable list of 171, which he considered relatively exhaustive. He called these *trait-elements*.

Now that he had his collection of things to be explained, the next step was to find out how they were related. Cattell had people rate other people on scales constructed from the list of 171 trait-elements and then intercorrelated all of the ratings. Each trait-element correlated high with some of the others and low with some. Just by looking at the patterns of intercorrelations, with some standard of what "high" and "low" meant, it was apparent that several groups, or clusters, had been obtained. Inside each cluster, correlations tended to be high, while trait-elements outside that cluster generally correlated low with those inside. Cattell found around 40 such clusters, which he called *surface traits*. Surface traits are groups of more or less interchangeable trait-elements which are used to describe individuals.

Cattell's real interest, of course, was not in surface traits. He wanted the underlying dimensions or *source traits*. These, in his view, were the necessities of rigorous scientific prediction. The clusters of trait-elements would be roughly comparable to clusters of cities and towns in our example above, such as the tightly packed clusters around New York or Los Angeles. Cattell wanted the dimensions, such as "North-South." Factor analysis gave him about 15 of these dimensions of personality space. In other words: The basic structure of personality in terms of behavior ratings has about 15 dimensions (source traits).

The whole process sounds easy, solid and scientific with clear results. But it would be a mistake to view mathematics—in this case, factor analysis—as the answer to our prayers for a thoroughly acceptable theory of personality. Like any mathematical technique, factor analysis is a tool.

It is sometimes likened to a meat grinder: You cannot put suet and bones into one end and come out with steak at the other. Note what Cattell put into the factor analysis—simple ratings of one person by another. These ratings are not very reliable. If the whole procedure were repeated with different raters or with different people to be rated, or even if you tried to replicate the first experiment, the ratings would vary somewhat, perhaps appreciably. Thus the intercorrelations would also be different, often quite different. Factor analysis would identify some dimensions not present before and would fail to find others that were found previously. Until what goes into the "meat grinder" is solid and scientific, what comes out can hardly claim to be THE theory of personality.

There are numerous other problems as well. One of these is the problem of knowing what we want to include in the personality sphere. The data in the above example were ratings of persons in lifelike situations. Cattell calls these *L-data* (life-record data), which also include other types of observations and countings. The number of accidental injuries per year, for example, is an L-datum. There are two other important broad categories of data in the personality sphere. *Q-data* (questionnaire data) are obtained by having a person rate himself or tell you what he feels ("I often feel lonely," "I would rather play poker than bridge"). *T-data* (test data) are derived from a person's performance on objective tests or in experimental situations. These three ways of gathering data, these *media,* have all been subjected to factor analysis. We noted around 15 factors or dimensions in L-data; Q-data have produced around 20; and T-data around 18, in addition to about 15 ability factors already identified by other researchers. The assumption is that eventually the "true" dimensions of personality will exhibit themselves in all three media—that is, that the same factors or source traits will emerge. The matching of content across media, however, is a delicate problem, with formidable theoretical and statistical obstacles.

We have yet to discuss what one does with these source traits once they have been obtained. Cattell's ultimate goal is to use them to predict behavior, employing what is called a *specification equation:*

$$Response = s_1 T_1 + s_2 T_2 + \ldots + s_n T_n$$

In other words, the response of an individual is predicted from the degree to which he exhibits each source trait T modified by the importance of the trait for that response, s. The response is one element in that great collection, the personality space, with which we started our analysis. The s values, at least average s values, are given by factor analysis. In our physical space example, a given response is analogous to a given city. Anchorage, Alaska, is so many miles (s_1) North (T_1)

and so many miles (s_2) West (T_2) of you. In like fashion, a response that will lead a person to be rated as "aggressive" has a unique location defined by a certain number of standardized units on each of the personality dimensions.

In predicting the behavior of an individual, we need to know how much of each trait he possesses. Assume, for the moment, that academic performance AP is predictable from two source traits called intelligence I and motivation M. Then $AP = s_1I + s_2M$. Assume also that intelligence is more important for this behavior than motivation. We might then have an expression such as $AP = .7I + .3M$. Now, in order to predict AP for an individual, we need to know *his* intelligence and *his* motivation. Psychological tests can be used to obtain an estimate of his endowment in each area. Once you know what the dimensions (source traits) *are*, you try to develop tests which provide a relatively pure measure of each dimension. Cattell has several tests on the market of this type, most notably the "16 PF" (16 Personality Factor Questionnaire), but we cannot discuss them here.

In the specification equation, Cattell has a definition of personality. His stated definition is this: "Personality is that which permits a prediction of what a person will do in a given situation" (1950, p. 2). It is clear that Cattell regards source traits as "that which permits a prediction." The T's in the specification equation are the dimensions of personality, and each person's standing on each of these dimensions constitutes that person's unique personality.

THE THEORY

Most of what we have discussed so far is closely tied to the technique of factor analysis. It is theory, of course, in the sense of telling us how to predict behavior. And it is even more deserving of the label "theory" because Cattell's search for basic dimensions was directed at all points by considerations of what kinds of tests, ratings, and so forth were important for personality theorists. He did not collect all sorts of measures indiscriminately, such as number of cavities over 6 months old, and so forth. An example of such directionality is his L-data sequence of analyses, which started with those attributes Allport and Odbert had compiled as important for personality research.

This section, however, concerns itself with some of the constructs and considerations that influence personality theorizing whether or not the theorist influenced uses the factor-analytic technique. We will be speaking hereafter almost entirely about source traits; "trait" will therefore mean "source trait" in the following.

Cattell makes several distinctions between kinds of traits. *Environment mold traits* have their source in the environment, in the society and the culture in which we live; they are learned. *Constitutional traits* have their source within the organism; they may be inherited, they may be innate physiological mechanisms. They may even change over time, as with maturation, but they do not reflect environmental pressures in the same way that environment mold traits do.

Other distinctions are between *ability* traits, *temperament* traits, and *dynamic* traits. Dynamic traits are most clearly motivational; they involve goal direction and behavior that varies as its incentive varies. Ability traits "are shown by *how well* the person makes his way to the accepted goals" (1950, p. 35). They involve behavior which varies as the complexity or difficulty of the task varies. Temperamental traits are what is left—that is, traits unaffected by incentive or complexity, such as "high-strungness." (Allport would call these expressive traits.)

Cattell's major theoretical contributions have centered on dynamic traits in combination with the presumed origin of the trait. Constitutional dynamic traits are called *ergs*, and environment mold traits are called *engrams* (structures in memory). The basic drives, or ergs, include sex, gregariousness, parental protectiveness, exploration or curiosity, escape, self-assertion, and others. Engrams (irregularly called metaergs), most of which are generalized attitudes or *sentiments*, include one's feelings for his profession, religion, and self (the self-sentiment) on a general level and the many different attitudes and interests of an individual on a more specific level.

The relationships between attitudes and interests, sentiments, and ergs are expressed in terms of *dynamic subsidiation,* a concept taken from Murray. Subsidiation means that one dynamic component of behavior is subordinate to another. To put money in the bank is a motive subsidiary (subordinate) to providing for family, a motive which in turn is subsidiary to sexual and parental needs. One can trace the line of subsidiation by asking "Why?" over and over as the subject expresses his attitudes or motives. For example, you want to put some money in your savings account. "Why?" Because I want to provide for my family. "Why do you want to provide for your family?" Because a family is an institution that enables me to fulfill certain basic needs, such as raising children, satisfying sexual desires, and so forth. Sooner or later, the answers stop coming ("I don't know") or at least stop making sense, as would probably be the case following the last question above. Theoretically, we will at this point have reached the most basic level, the level of ergs, which are explained in terms of the nature of the beast. "In human behavior where reason ends, instinct begins" (1950, p. 156).

In practice, the chain of subsidiation is a great deal more complex than we have indicated above. You may put money in the bank (specific interest or attitude) for a number of more basic reasons (sentiments), and the sentiment for family is basic to a number of attitudes as well as subordinate to a number of even more basic ergs. This complex interaction of attitudes, sentiments, and ergs is called the *dynamic lattice*. It is a term whose function now is largely to indicate the complexity with which the factor analyst must deal, but it has the capability of becoming a realistic diagram of an individual's dynamic components when more research makes this feasible.

SUMMARY

The power of mathematics in formulating and using a theory has been demonstrated in the physical sciences. In the social sciences, however, and even among mathematicians, much controversy has centered on the desirability of techniques such as factor analysis. There is no question that such techniques are often applied blindly and inappropriately, with results that are somehow impressive but meaningless. On the other hand, when regarded as a tool rather than a panacea, sophisticated mathematical approaches can illuminate many areas of ignorance in personology. If you are interested in a relationship between two variables, and you assume you have measured those two variables in an adequate fashion (on an adequate scale with good validity), the relationship described mathematically is far more useful than if represented otherwise. The problem of adequately formulating constructs and scales is the real pitfall; but even here, mathematical techniques (if used correctly) can be utilized to identify deficiencies and problems. If Cattell's theory is inadequate in present form, it may yet form the shoulders on which a better formulation may stand.

The future development of factor-analytic theories will probably be determined, as will the future of all theories, by advancement in the thought of personologists on the nature of efficient and effective constructs. The trait approach has led to some difficulties in whatever form it takes; Allport and Cattell are examples of this. Traits as presently thought of do not appear to account for much variation in human behavior (Mischel, 1968). If there are problems in the measures and in the conceptualization, the output from factor analysis cannot be expected to be problem-free.

While the existence of these problems is clear, their solutions are not. In future attempts to solve them, some personologists will try more sophisticated conceptualizations of surface and source traits, of ergs and engrams, and of dynamic lattices. Others will abandon traits and turn to different types of constructs (see, for an example, Chapter 8). Improved techniques, both in factor analysis and in test construction, will be useful for any type of construct. Whatever the outcome, Cattell will have made a contribution to it.

REFERENCES

Allport, G. W., & Odbert, H. S. Trait-names: A psycho-lexical study. *Psychological Monographs*, 1936, **47**, No. 211.

Cattell, R. B. *Description and measurement of personality*. New York: World Book Co., 1946.

Cattell, R. B. *Personality: A systematic, theoretical, and factual study*. New York: McGraw-Hill, 1950.

Cattell, R. B. *Personality and motivation structure and measurement*. New York: Harcourt, Brace & World, 1957.

Cattell, R. B. Personality theory growing from multivariate quantitative research. In S. Koch (Ed.), *Psychology: A study of a science*. Vol. III. New York: McGraw-Hill, 1959.

Mischel, W. *Personality and assessment*. New York: Wiley, 1968.

The adjective most fitting for the personality theory of Neal Miller and John Dollard is "integrative." Miller had long been respected for his work in the area of experimental learning theory, while Dollard's expertise lay in the field of modern social science: social psychology, sociology, and cultural anthropology. In a series of books, they integrated these two lines of thought into a coherent theory of personality founded on basic principles of learning in the context of the "social conditions under which human beings learn" (1950, p. 3). It is a social learning theory with an assist from the genius of Freud, Lewin, and other theorists; the important dynamic events in the life history of the individual, as identified by these other personologists, are translated into the terminology of Miller and Dollard.

After treating the fundamentals of the social learning theory and some of its implications, we will examine the contribution of these theorists in three problem areas where their influence has been considerable: imitation, conflict, and frustration-aggression.

SOCIAL LEARNING THEORY

The analysis of learning relies on four basic constructs: *drive, cue, response,* and *reinforcement.* Drives provide the "push," or motivation, for response; cues direct the behavior; and reinforcement strengthens the bond between the cue and the response. This bond might be considered a fifth basic construct, since it is the bond that is "learned" and the strength of the bond indicates the degree of learning that has occurred.

Consider a man driven by hunger. He sees a vending machine (cue). He inserts a coin and pulls a lever (responses). Out falls a candy bar which he eats and which, for a time, satisfies his hunger (reinforcement). The theory suggests that the bond between the cue and the responses has been strengthened because the man received the reinforcement, hence he is more likely to insert a coin and pull the lever of the vending machine the next time he is hungry. In somewhat more technical terms, a drive is considered "strong stimulation" that "impels the subject to act or respond" (1950, p. 29). Reinforcement is defined in related terms; it is anything that reduces the strong stimulation of the drive, as food reduces the strong internal stimulation of hunger.

Like drives, cues are stimuli. They are stimuli which are not intense enough to motivate but yet strong enough to direct behavior. In theories of personality we must be prepared to deal with complex cues such as spatial or temporal patterns of stimuli (e.g., "vending machine" or "mother"). Human language facilitates this task by assigning single, discriminable labels to these complex patterns. Response, too, is a complex term when used in the study of personality. Miller and Dollard use the term *response hierarchy* to suggest that typically a cue is linked (bonded) with not one but rather with several different responses, which themselves may be quite complex. At any given time, a cue will usually elicit that response to which its bonding is greatest, that is, the person will behave in the way that has undergone the greatest amount of learning. In some cases there may be an unlearned (innate) response to a cue that has a stronger bond than any learned response.

Learning is to be considered not so much the learning of a single response as, rather, a change in the response hierarchy. Such a change (in which a less prominent response assumes the most prominent position in the hierarchy) is unlikely unless a person finds himself in a situation in which his previously effective responses are of no avail. Such a situation Miller and Dollard call a *learning dilemma*; it is here that significant learning occurs.

Before continuing this discussion, we must introduce some additional terms. *Extinction* of a response is almost the opposite of learning. Extinction occurs when a response is repeated without reinforcement, and it is indicated by a decrease of the tendency to perform the response. If the hungry man in our example were to find, as is all too often the case, that the infernal vending machine consistently took his money and gave him nothing in return, then the response of inserting money and pulling the lever would soon extinguish. The next day, however, it may be that our hero is willing to risk a few more coins in the machine before giving up entirely. The reappearance of the response after its extinction is called *spontaneous recovery*. It suggests that at least some temporary inhibition of the response is present in extinction, that extinction is not the exact opposite of learning (destruction vs. construction of the bond).

Generalization and *discrimination* are two principles related to each other. Generalization refers to the transfer of a learned response from one cue to a similar cue. Our example might insert a coin into a different vending machine once he had learned that the first gave satisfactory reinforcement. If, however, of four machines in the building only one was in working order, he would soon learn to *discriminate* good machines from bad. The process of discrimination would probably involve reinforcement by one machine and generalization to the others, thus leading him to respond to machines giving no reinforcement, resulting in the extinction of his response to them but not to the first. Discrimination will then have occurred.

Another basic principle is called *delay of reinforcement;* it indicates that reinforcement is the more effective the closer it follows the response. How long a period can elapse between response and reinforcement without eliminating learning is a vigorously debated issue in learning theory, with many theorists suggesting that even a second's delay is too long. Whatever the answer, this principle causes us to focus on *secondary reinforcements,* or *learned rewards,* in human behavior, since it is rare in everyday life that a response is followed directly by reward. A secondary reinforcement is a stimulus that has been repeatedly associated with primary reinforcement. A dinner bell, for example, may serve as a secondary reinforcement because of its repeated association with the primary reinforcement of food. In everyday life, man works (behaves) for long hours without primary reinforcement of his basic hunger, thirst, sex, or pain-avoidance drives; many theorists feel that it is money (a secondary reinforcement associated with several different primary reinforcements) or perhaps the thought of money that serves to bridge the gap between behavior and ultimate reward.

The counterpart of secondary reinforcement is *secondary motivation,* or *learned drive.* Just as previously neutral stimuli come to serve as rewards through their association with primary reinforcements, stimuli commonly associated with drives come to acquire motivating properties of their own. The most extensively studied of the learned drives is fear, which is elicited by stimuli associated with pain. In a classic experiment by Miller (1948), rats were electrically shocked for a number of trials in a white compartment; they escaped by running to a black compartment. Later, when the shocks were discontinued, the rats continued to escape when placed in the white compartment. To show that a drive was involved and not merely a response of running into the black compartment, Miller then closed the door between the two compartments. The motivated rats quickly learned that by rotating a small wheel they could open the door and escape.

HIGHER MENTAL PROCESSES

Although the paradigm of social learning presented above can be applied directly to simple learning situations, an understanding of human behavior requires its extension to those most human of charactertistics, thought and language. This extension does not require new principles but does require a close look at the nature of thought and language, the way they are learned, and the way they are used. It is the contention of Dollard and Miller that thought (mental words, sentences, or images) can be considered a response. Hence thoughts that are followed by reinforcement become bonded to cues just as behaviors do. Thoughts, however, fulfill a peculiar function in the organized behavior sequence. Dollard and Miller (1950) call them "cue-producing responses." Thoughts "produce a cue that is part of the stimulus pattern leading to another response" (1950, p. 98). A simple example that illustrates the process is mental counting. Suppose you buy something for $4.89 and pay for it with a five-dollar bill. The clerk gives you your change in pennies. As they are received, you count to yourself, "One, two, three, . . ." The last number will determine which of the following verbal responses is to be made: "O.K.," "too much," or "too little." The thought produces a cue that leads to the next response.

Language often has a similar function in that it produces cues, rather than effects any change in the environment. Although swearing at another person might be considered an instrumental response or even a drive-satisfying response, it is often useful to view swearing as a cue since there are few better ways of getting a response from your target. Language also aids in the generalization or discrimination of things or events not usually seen as similar or different. Although a dime plus a penny, two nickels plus a penny, and eleven pennies are not easily seen as identical, it would have made no difference to you which set of coins the clerk had given you in the above example. By labeling through language, there is a learned equivalence among the sets. Conversely, it would be extremely difficult to discriminate between 100 pennies in a pile and 99 pennies in another pile, but the labels "one dollar" and "99 cents," are clearly discriminable.

Language allows for considerable economy in the complex interactions that constitute human society. Very often a word is the stimulus associated with a primary drive or reinforcement. A cry of *"Fire!"* in a crowded theater has long been accorded its due motivating power, and the written word EXIT in such a case becomes a strong incentive. Foresight, reasoning, and the like all rely heavily on the powerful effects of thoughts, words, and images. ("What would happen if I . . . ?") The difficulty of training a very young child, Dollard and Miller (1950) suggest, is due largely to the fact that young children cannot respond to verbal cues given by others or themselves. "One cannot reason with them" (1950, p. 107).

IMITATION

One of the major problems to which the social learning theory was applied was that of imitation: what it is, how it occurs, and how it is learned. In their 1941 book, Miller and Dollard distinguish three classes of imitative behavior. The first they call *same behavior*. It consists of two people viewing the same cue and making the same response. Each had learned the response independently.

The second class of imitative behavior is called *matched-dependent behavior*. The response in "same behavior" could be performed without a second person being present (although, of course, it thereby loses its designation as "imitative"), but matched-dependent behavior requires a pair, or dyad. Matched-dependent behavior usually occurs in situations in which it is reasonable to identify one person as leader and the other as follower. The leader notes an environmental cue and makes a response. The follower makes the same or similar response, but his response is elicited by cues from the leader, not by cues from the environment. A foreman in a mine may be showing me around when he hears faint cracking noises and begins to run for the surface. Although my untrained ears do not detect the noises or do not assign any importance to them, I run for my life nevertheless. What elicits my running is the sight of the foreman running.

Matched-dependent behavior is easy to see in children, especially when there is an age difference in the pair. The older child hears a car drive up, then goes to the door to meet the gift-bearing father. The younger child does the same, but does so because he sees the older child doing it. He has yet to associate the screeching sounds in the environment with the prospect of some candy. Imitation, here defined as matching, is a response; and it is associated with cues like any other response. The cues come from the leader, the response (matching) is made, and the reinforcement (candy) follows.

The third class of imitative behavior is called *copying*. One person attempts to make his response the same as that of another person. Copying commonly occurs in the training of skills (as when the fledgling pianist attempts to make his response identical with that of his teacher) and in behavior associated with social status (as when we watch the host to see which fork is used on the salad).

Copying involves learning to respond to perceptions of sameness and difference. Very often it is necessary to enlist the aid of an external critic (a teacher, for example) in order to learn this. The critic rewards same behaviors and punishes different responses, usually with verbal secondary reinforcements such as "good" or "that's not right." After considerable training the learner himself may be able to distinguish sameness and difference without the help of the teacher. New stimuli, associated with the teacher's rewards and punishments will have taken over; stimuli that, we hope, do not require the presence of the teacher.

Contrasting matched-dependent behavior with copying, Miller and Dollard state:

The essential difference between the two processes is that in matched-dependent behavior the imitator responds only to the cue from the leader, while in copying he responds only to the cues of sameness and difference produced by stimulation from his own and model's response (1941, p. 159).

Imitative behavior, once it is understood in terms of Miller and Dollard's theory, is viewed as a major element in human society and culture. In their 1941 book, Miller and Dollard go on to discuss the role of imitative behavior in crowd behavior and in the diffusion of culture.

DYNAMICS OF CONFLICT

Miller and Dollard, in particular Miller, have made an influential contribution to the social-learning analysis of conflict. Conflict is a main factor in almost every theory of personality, especially in theories of psychopathology. The term "conflict" is somewhat ambiguous and is used in different ways in different theories. Miller (1944) makes it clear that he uses "conflict" to mean "competition between incompatible responses" (p. 431). This definition means that we are dealing with intrapersonal conflict within a single individual instead of with conflict between persons.

Miller deals with two general response systems: to approach and to avoid. We "approach" food when we are hungry. We "avoid" pain. Miller lists four principles concerning approach, avoidance, and conflict. These principles are assumed to hold for most but not all cases.

1. The tendency to approach a goal is stronger the nearer the subject is to it. This is called the *approach gradient.*

2. The tendency to go away from a place or object avoided is stronger the nearer the subject is to it. This is called the *avoidance gradient.*

3. The strength of avoidance increases more rapidly with nearness than does the strength of approach. In other words, it may be said that the avoidance gradient is steeper than the approach gradient.

4. The strength of the tendencies to approach or avoid varies with the strength of the drive upon which the tendency is based. Thus, an increased drive may be said to raise the height of the entire gradient. (See Miller, 1944, pp. 433–434.)

While approach-avoidance conflict concepts were introduced by Lewin (see Chapter 10) prior to Miller's work, Miller's concepts are based on ingenious experimental work by Brown (1948). After training two groups of rats to either approach (food) or avoid (shock) one end of an experimental runway, Brown fitted the rats with small harnesses and restrained them close to the goal or far from the goal. The measure taken was the pulling force exerted by the rats at the two distances. The results are shown in Figure 2. In both cases, the pulling force was greater when measured closer to the goal (principles 1 and 2), although when avoiding, the rats were trying to get away from the goal and when approaching they were trying to reach it. The difference in pulling force between the near position and the far position was much greater for the avoidance response than for the approach response (principle 3).

Principle 4 was illustrated in similar fashion. Comparing the gradients for a group of rats trained with strong shock with those for a group trained with weaker shock, Brown found that the gradient between the far and near positions was the same (equally steep) but that the average pulling force at all positions was greater in the case of strong shock.

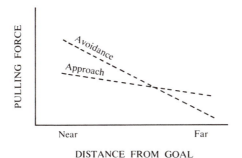

DISTANCE FROM GOAL

Figure 2

Relationship between motivation and distance from a goal. (From Neal E. Miller, "Experimental Studies of Conflict" in Personality and the Behavior Disorders, edited by J. McV. Hunt. Copyright 1944, The Ronald Press Company, New York.)

So far we have been discussing animals, each of which makes one of two different responses. Conflict, however, occurs when an animal wants to make both responses: he wants to approach, but he also wants to avoid. If such an animal could be represented by the gradients in Figure 2, we would expect him to approach when he is far away from the goal because at that point the approach response is dominant—that is, he pulls harder to approach than to avoid. If he were at the near position, we would expect him to avoid. In both cases we would expect him to run to the position indicated by the point at which the lines cross, that is, the point at which the two tendencies are equal. He should vacillate around that point. Miller (1944) describes experimental results that support this hypothesis.

The conflict between tendencies to approach and avoid is common in human behavior. Should I study tonight? I approach studying because it will lead to desired goals. On the other hand, I avoid studying because it is sometimes dull and boring. So what do I do? I vacillate, neither studying effectively nor doing anything else constructive.

How does one resolve this conflict? Two immediate answers stem from the principle which states that drive increases the height of the gradient. If you could increase the drive associated with approach, you might be able to raise the gradient of approach above that of avoidance at every point. Then there would be no point at which the two gradients cross, no point at which avoidance is stronger than approach, and therefore no point of vacillation. Similarly, you might try to decrease the drive associated with avoidance. Students often do this by means of thought-mediated drives. For example, they tell themselves that studying is extremely important or that it is really fun once you get going.

The type of conflict discussed so far has been named *approach-avoidance conflict*. There are other types of conflict, some resolved easily and some not so easily. For these we will have to consider two goals separated in space or in time or both. *Approach-approach conflict* means that one has a tendency to approach both goals. The philosopher's hungry ass is seen as positioned equidistant from two delicious piles of hay. A conflict of this type is easily resolved, for as soon as the ass moves one way or the other the approach gradient for the closer goal will exceed that of the farther and he will make his way merrily to his reward. *Avoidance-avoidance conflict*, on the other hand, is neither pleasant nor easy to resolve. If a person with such a conflict cannot "drop out" (leave the field of conflict), he usually vacillates at the spatial or temporal center, where the tendency to avoid one goal is equal to the tendency to avoid the other. Moving toward one goal increases the tendency to avoid that one, and so the person moves back to the vacillation point.

Vacillation also occurs in the final type of conflict, *double approach-avoidance*, so named because each of the goals elicits a tendency to approach and to avoid. The nearer one approaches a goal, the greater the increase in one's tendency to avoid that goal; the farther one gets from the goal, the greater the increase in one's tendency to approach it. Hence the resultant tendency to approach Goal A (approach minus avoidance) is the less, the closer one gets to Goal A; and the resultant tendency to approach Goal B increases as one gets closer to

Goal A. Again, a point might be reached at which the tendency to approach A equals the tendency to approach B, and vacillation would occur at this point.

There is a theoretical rationale for the assumption that the avoidance gradient is steeper than the approach gradient. Either gradient is seen as a function of the stimulus-similarity of a given position to the goal. The farther one is from the goal, the less similar are the stimuli to the stimuli at the goal; hence the declining gradients in both cases. These stimuli, however, include both external and internal stimuli. Fear of shock (avoidance) is triggered mostly by stimuli that are external, or environmental. Hunger (approach) is triggered mostly by internal stimuli. Consequently, hunger can be expected to be less different between the near and far positions than fear and also to have an approach gradient less steep than the avoidance gradient of fear. There is no intrinsic reason for the avoidance gradient to be steeper than the approach gradient; under proper conditions, the reverse may even occur. Miller (1944) mentions one experiment in which the whole length of the runway was electrified, rather than just one end. The slope of the avoidance gradient was much flatter than it typically is.

FRUSTRATION AND AGGRESSION

The exploration of the relationship between frustration and aggression was the first joint effort of Dollard and Miller. In collaboration with L. W. Doob, O. H. Mowrer, and R. R. Sears they sought to explore the hypothesis

that aggression is always a consequence of frustration. More specifically the proposition is that the occurrence of aggressive behavior always presupposes the existence of frustration and, contrariwise, that the existence of frustration always leads to some form of aggression (1939, p. 1).

Frustration is defined as interference with an "instigated goal-response at its proper time in the behavior sequence" (Dollard et al., 1939, p. 7). Instigated here means essentially *driven;* that is, the behavior that the goal-response is part of is motivated by some primary or learned *drive.* If I am hungry, I am instigated to reach for food. If you stop me from reaching, you have interfered; I am frustrated. Aggression is defined as any "sequence of behavior, the goal-response to which is the injury of the person toward whom it is directed" (1939, p. 9). This definition excludes accidental injuries; *intention* to do harm is a necessary component.

The simple hypothesis that frustration leads to aggression is by no means a new idea. As we have seen in other sections of this chapter (for example on conflict), what makes Miller and Dollard influential in personality research is not the restatement of a relationship that has been discussed by many others but rather the form in which it is cast. The relatively precise definitions, the translation into stimulus-and-response terminology which many find more workable when doing experimental research, the creative amplification of the implications within the framework of stimulus-response theory: these are the factors that have made the frustration-aggression hypothesis one that no theorist interested in aggression can afford to overlook. He may disagree with it, but he cannot overlook it.

Let us look at some of the details of this hypothesis. What can we say about the degree of aggression that will be exhibited? According to the hypothesis, it should depend on the degree of frustration. On what does frustration depend? It should depend on the degree of "instigation" to the goal-response that is interfered with. Since drive is a major component of instigation, we can study this conjecture directly. For example, interfering with the attempt of a hungry animal to get food should elicit aggression. Interfering with an animal starved for 48 hours should elicit more aggression than interfering with one who has been kept 12 hours without food.

The degree of interference should also be a factor, and if one assumes that frustration builds up, the number of frustration sequences must also be considered. These notions have been tested by many researchers in the laboratory, and they can be put to a crude test in society as well. Hovland and Sears (1940), for example, assumed that the price of cotton in any given year could be used as an index of the degree of interference with the goal of making money for Southern farmers. They found a strong relationship between the price of cotton and the number of lynchings (aggression) over a period of years: when the cotton price went down, the victims went up.

Needless to say, aggressive behavior may be any of a number of acts. In addition, aggressive behavior of a direct nature can be inhibited. For example, if a would-be aggressor expects punishment or the failure of a planned attack, then the aggressive behavior may not occur. If the frustrating agent happens to be a loved one, inhibition of direct attack is likely.

Aggression is directed toward the object or person that is perceived to be the source of frustration. The degree of aggression defines a class of appropriate attacks. If inhibition occurs, the degree of aggression may be lessened, or the object of aggression may be changed. The first of these possibilities is derived from the basic principle of satisfaction. The angry mother feels like hitting, but merely reprimands her errant child. Half a loaf is better than none.

If the object of aggression is such that no reasonable act of aggression is possible, the frustrated individual may vent his anger on another object. The selection of the other object or person is thought to be determined by the principle of generalization. That object which is most similar in some way to the primary target will be attacked; if the secondary target is also impossible, the next most similar object will be attacked. Frustrated by his father, a son may swear at a policeman, who has the same sex role and authority status as his impervious father.

Aggression against oneself is not uncommon in our society. It is easy to trace the origins of self-aggression, which may arise in two ways. First, it may be that the self is perceived as the cause of interference, which is certainly common enough in many goal-directed activities. "I failed": the self, through lack of ability, has become the cause of frustration. Second, if the cause of interference is other than the self, the resulting aggressive impulse may be inhibited; aggression, goal-directed activity like any other, is thus thwarted *by the self*. The aggression then "turns against the self." Self-aggression is usually inhibited since one is not likely to injure a "loved one"! Interfering with the aggressive drive thus produces more frustration and more aggression against the self, which in turn is inhibited. A vicious circle of self-aggression, frustration, and more aggression is set up. Severe depression or suicide may ultimately follow.

Dollard et al. (1939) go on to give many examples and statistics from the field of crime, political systems, and anthropology, among others. Since the publication of this book, there have been some revisions in the frustration-aggression hypothesis by the authors, mainly in the direction of weakening the strength of the proposed relationship. In its strong form, as in the quotation introducing this section, the hypothesis states that where there is frustration there is always aggression and vice versa. In the weaker form of the hypothesis, there is seen a relationship between frustration and aggression, but the relationship is not perfect. Dollard and Miller, for example, state that "the hypothesis put forward here . . . is that the position aggression will occupy in the initial hierarchy of responses to any situation is largely a product of learning" (1950, p. 84). In other words, aggression is largely a learned response to frustration, and people will vary in the degree of this learning. It appears, however, that aggression is a response likely to be learned because of the nature of people or of society. A theorist may look at other possible responses to frustration, but he had better consider aggression too.

SUMMARY

The Miller-Dollard theory is a social-learning approach to personality. It is also an example of integration between personology and learning theory. Integrations are always popular and always difficult. To find two "skills" represented by two fine scholars who can work together is rare, and such an effort must therefore be seriously considered in the history of a discipline.

As in all such integrations, the chief advantage is gained from the marriage of the strengths of each area. Personality theory had the content of importance but lacked concepts suitable for rigorous experimentation. Learning theories had developed such concepts, more so than personology anyway, but their contents tended to be too specific and narrow for application across the full range of human behavior. To combine content with concepts and method is a desired goal. The extent to which Miller and Dollard achieved this goal is a judgment best left to history; the attempt in itself is noteworthy.

Miller and Dollard's research on various "old" issues in personality is also important. Before being translated into the language of experimental learning theory, many of these problems were relatively impervious to empirical study. Imitation, intrapersonal conflict, and frustration-aggression are topics which today occupy a significant percentage of space in research journals. Miller and Dollard deserve much of the credit.

If there is a general "fault" in the attempted integration, it is that the research from the Miller-Dollard theory remained somewhat nonsocial. For example, experimentation on animals was perhaps too easily generalized to human behavior. We shall see in the next chapter a criticism on this basis. But perhaps this fault is not so much a fault as rather an almost necessary accompaniment of the early stages of such integrative effort. One should not criticize youth for being too young.

REFERENCES

Brown, J. S. Gradients of approach and avoidance responses and their relation to motivation. *Journal of Comparative and Physiological Psychology*, 1948, **41**, 450–465.

Dollard, J., Doob, L. W., Miller, N. E., Mowrer, O. H., & Sears, R. R. *Frustration and aggression*. New Haven, Conn.: Yale Univ. Press, 1939.

Dollard, J., & Miller, N. E. *Personality and psychotherapy*. New York: Mc-Graw-Hill, 1950.

Hovland, C. I., & Sears, R. R. Minor studies of aggression: VI. Correlations of lynchings with economic indices. *Journal of Psychology*, 1940, **9**, 301–310.

Miller, N. E. Experimental studies of conflict. In J. McV. Hunt (Ed.), *Personality and the behavior disorders*. Vol. I. New York: Ronald Press, 1944.

Miller, N. E. Theory and experiment relating psychoanalytic displacement to stimulus response generalization. *Journal of Abnormal and Social Psychology*, 1948, **43**, 155–178.

Miller, N. E. Liberalization of basic S-R concepts. In S. Koch (Ed.), *Psychology: A study of a science*. Vol. II. New York: McGraw-Hill, 1959.

Miller, N. E., & Dollard, J. *Social learning and imitation*. New Haven, Conn.: Yale Univ. Press, 1941.

ALBERT BANDURA AND RICHARD WALTERS

Every personality theory has as its goal the explanation of *human social behavior,* and in one way or another every personality theory deals with *learning.* It is therefore somewhat surprising to encounter what is clearly a new and different approach, that of Bandura and Walters (1963), which claims as its two most distinctive characteristics a focus on human social behavior and an emphasis on learning. The implication here, of course, is that other theories do not deal adequately with these phenomena. The explicit designation as a learning theory, for example, implies a criticism of trait and psychoanalytic theories for their inability to predict and control behavior in a precise and rigorous fashion. Other theories which make this criticism, such as Miller and Dollard's, are in turn viewed by Bandura and Walters as lacking proper emphasis on human behavior in social contexts because they utilize evidence from nonhuman studies—animal experiments—or from human but nonsocial research, such as individuals learning lists of words.

The Bandura-Walters social learning theory of personality emphasizes precise experimentation dealing with human subjects and with processes relevant to and often tested in interpersonal settings. The content of the theory is mostly empirically derived principles of learning, performance, and behavior modification. The theory is largely contained in a vast series of individually reported studies made by Bandura, Walters, their associates, and others. Much of the early research is reviewed in Bandura and Walters (1963), and Bandura's 1969 book, *Principles of Behavioral Modification,* summarizes many of the subsequent studies. Even with two excellent summaries, however, a theory of this nature defies brief description; we can only hope to glimpse the basic approach by means of a sparse sampling of illustrative experiments.

A SOCIAL LEARNING APPROACH

The social learning approach used by Bandura and Walters focuses on (1) the behavior in question, and (2) the mechanisms by which this behavior is established and regulated. To describe behavior in adequate fashion is by no means an easy task. First, the description must avoid any implication of an explanatory mechanism. To say that Jack murdered Joe, for example, implies (in the word murdered) several things that are not observable in the behavior itself: an intent to kill, the absence of customs legalizing such behavior (such as war), and so forth. Second, certain values in our culture, such as education, creativity, and "personal growth," are obviously related to behaviors, but to behaviors that are not easily identified or categorized. In general, since language itself inevitably involves some degree of abstraction and probably needs some "sloppiness" (flexibility) to fulfill its function, words used to describe behavior will always miss the mark to varying degrees.

One needn't despair of scientific gain, however, as long as phrases like "personal growth" abound. Any specification of behavior is bound to improve on such a designation. More salient is the second focus of the approach: the kinds of establishing and regulating mechanisms. Many personality theories—psychoanalytic and trait theories in particular—place heavy stress on hypothetical internal states of the person. These states are usually conceived of as relatively stable, enduring, and general. The social learning approach, on the other hand, emphasizes three distinct classes of mechanisms (Bandura, 1969). Some behaviors, especially emotional behaviors, are primarily under the mechanism or *external stimulus control*. The second class of mechanisms is *feedback*: rewards and punishments or, more generally, "outcome" information. Behaviors established by feedback mechanisms often can be controlled by external stimuli too, when those stimuli signify probable consequences. The third class is *central mediational processes*, which refer to self-generated stimulation that is relatively independent of environmental events. Bandura and Walters have frequently criticized the inferential variables of psychodynamic and trait theorists as improperly formulated and used. These criticisms have caused many to overlook the major role of inferential variables in the social learning approach. Self-reinforcement (internal) operations, for example, are commonly discussed and researched; and vicarious or observational learning, in which a subject learns by watching another person, is another topic of major importance for which stimulus and outcome (for the subject) play little role.

It is difficult to distinguish between the approach of Bandura and Walters and that of Miller and Dollard. The theories share a distaste for what they see as imprecise conceptualization and experimentation in traditional approaches; they share, too, a learning orientation, and their concepts are taken largely from this orientation as it has developed in the course of animal experimentation. Some of the distinctions that could be made between them have to do with technical and historical matters of little concern to the beginning student. Perhaps the clearest and most relevant distinction has been indicated above in the discussion of the terms "human" and "social" as adjectives preceding "learning" in the theory of Bandura and Walters.

Miller and Dollard, in the opinion of Bandura and Walters, are often misled by generalizing from animal or human nonsocial learning principles. An instructive example of this criticism is given in a discussion of *displacement of aggression*. Displacement was originally a psychoanalytic term which referred to the defensive tendency to aggress against someone or something other than the person or thing that offends you. The true object of your aggression may be too powerful or prestigious to attack directly. A child, for instance, may be provoked by his parents, but direct aggression against them might lead to painful punishment. He therefore goes out into the neighborhood and becomes highly aggressive there.

The question is: Toward what in the neighborhood does he become aggressive? Is there some way of predicting the object or person upon which the original aggression will be displaced? Miller and Dollard suggest that displacement will occur along a dimension of stimulus similarity, that the stimulus object most similar to the original object will be attacked. If that response must also be suppressed, then the next most similar stimulus will be the object of aggression. This nonsocial explanation, in Bandura and Walters' words,

ignores the influence of the original agents of frustration . . . in determining responses toward stimulus objects other than themselves. In fact, parents often through precept, example, and control of reinforcement . . . determine rather precisely the . . . displaced responses. . . . Displaced aggression is further modified by the response it elicits from other socializing agents and from the objects of aggression themselves. Miller's generalization gradients thus become relatively meaningless for a human-learning situation in which the patterns of reward-punishment . . . displayed by parents and other agents of socialization have no consistent relationship to the similarity of the parents to possible objects of aggression (1963, pp. 19–20).

The main points in this quotation are that in human social situations (1) we are dealing with people who are in the business of influencing the behaviors of others, and (2) the social influence rarely coincides with simple physical dimensions such as stimulus similarity. The frustrated boy is taught where he can safely aggress and where he cannot, and information on his "education" in these matters is a far superior predictor of the object of aggression than stimulus similarity. He may go out and attack a Negro, for example, because he has been taught that aggression against Negroes is acceptable, even desirable. To assume that a black man has more perceived characteristics in common with his aggression-provoking white mother than any other acceptable target strains the limits of credulity, not to mention the conflict of such a similarity interpretation with perceptual discrimination theories of prejudice.

Thus, it is the feeling of Bandura and Walters that we cannot simply translate principles from animal and nonsocial learning theories and thereby create a viable personality theory. The principles so obtained may indeed be a fruitful source of hypotheses, but they must be tested, extended, modified. The acceptable principles are those emerging from experimental evidence concerning human social interaction.

The empirical results of this approach (findings and principles which by and large *are* the theory) will be explored in three areas: 1. Modeling, which deals with the acquisition of behavior.   2. The effects of reinforcement and punishment.   3. Techniques for behavior modification.

MODELING

Modeling is the term that has replaced *imitation* in later versions of the theory (Bandura, 1969) primarily because modeling encompasses a wider range of phenomena. In this process, one person (the model) does something and another watches the behavior. The observer may then reproduce the behavior in very specific detail, which is the narrower meaning usually assigned to imitation. What the observer "reproduces," in other cases, may be similar to the model's behavior only along some abstract conceptual dimension—morality, for example. If a number of models are observed (perhaps the more typical state of affairs in "real life"), then the observer's behavior is likely to be some combination of elements from the various models (Bandura, Ross, and Ross, 1963). And in some cases, performance of similar behavior may not occur at all, either through unattentive observation or lack of positive incentive.

One of the primary functions of modeling in the theory is to explain the emergence of novel behaviors. The behavior of an adult human, for example, cannot easily be predicted from his activities as a child. Learning plays such a major role in human behavior that it is sometimes difficult to see how certain enormously complex skills (building a house, writing a book) could ever have developed. Most of the responses by adults can be called novel or new, in the sense that they are not observable earlier in life. How these novel responses develop is one of the most important questions for a theory of personality, yet neither personality theories nor learning theories have dealt effectively with it. Instead these theories have focused on how behaviors already present are increased or decreased in frequency through reinforcement, punishment, or extinction (withdrawal of reinforcement).

One very notable exception is Skinner's (1953) notion of *successive approximations*. Basically, this notion describes a procedure in which a response already available is gradually changed by rewarding certain aspects until the final form of behavior is quite different. To train a rat to dance, for example, one begins by rewarding any elevation of the rat's head above its normal position. As the rat starts raising his head to get the reward, further "demands" are made on his talents: He must raise his head higher, and higher yet, until finally he must stand up to get the reward. Once you have him standing, you can begin a similar procedure, gradually increasing the degree of body turn the rat must accomplish before he receives his food pellet. Eventually, the standing, spinning rat will elicit amazed cries of "Look! He dances!" from spectators, especially if you have taken care to teach the rat that such responses are rewarded only when music is playing.

The method of successive approximations will result in novel responses; it is an effective and perfectly respectable procedure. Whether all novel human behavior can be attributed to learning by successive approximations, however, is doubtful. There is considerable evidence that many novel responses are produced by imitation or modeling. The fact that observational learning exists justified the conclusion that successive approximation is not the sole underlying process. In addition, modeling is apparently a much quicker process (Bandura and McDonald, 1963); the enormously complex behavior systems of adults must be highly dependent on the resulting efficiency (economy of effort).

Imitation, as we have seen, was strongly emphasized in the theory of Miller and Dollard (Chapter 7). The Miller-Dollard formulation, however, does not use imitation to explain novel behaviors. Rather, they concern themselves mostly with the occurrence of pre-existing responses in new situations—for example, a young child imitating the running-to-door response of an older sibling when the latter hears their father approaching. The failure to deal adequately with the acquisition of novel behavior is viewed by Bandura and Walters as a deficiency which they propose to remedy.

In the Bandura-Walters formulation, the acquisition of novel responses through modeling is illustrated by an experiment in which nursery school children observed adult models who exhibited *unusual* types of aggressive behavior toward a large plastic doll. These children showed a greater frequency of *precisely imitative* aggressive responses than did control subjects who did not observe the models (Bandura, Ross, and Ross, 1961). The presence of relatively novel behaviors ("unusual") and the replication of these novel behaviors ("precisely imitative") show the effect to be imitation rather than simple triggering of aggression (see *disinhibition,* below).

In line with their intended focus on behavior rather than on highly abstract theoretical constructs, once the basic phenomenon of imitative learning had been demonstrated, Bandura and Walters set out to discover the situational and personal determinants of behavior. Does the model have to be live? No. Models on film and even cartoon characters work well. Whom will people imitate? They will imitate models whom they perceive as somehow similar to themselves more than models seen as dissimilar. Are some people more likely to imitate? Yes. Persons more likely to imitate are those with histories of insufficient reward for personal initiative and those who have been frequently rewarded for imitation in the past. If the modeled behavior includes a reaction to the environment or to other persons, does this make a difference? Yes. If a model is rewarded for its behavior, the subject is more likely to perform the same behavior—but the learning of the behavior appears to be independent of reward or punishment.

The above findings illustrate the Bandura-Walters approach. Apart from a few basic concepts, the theory consists largely of a set of principles derived from numerous experiments. The experimentation is composed of systematic variations in components of the fundamental phenomenon: characteristics of the model, characteristics of the observer, characteristics of the modeling situation. In other words, it is very much an empirical approach, in which modeling is studied under all these conditions to see whether the original effect persists and to what degree. Later developments in the theory (Bandura, 1969) have been more concerned with central mediational processes. And one of the prime effects (or causes?) of this concern is the extension of the modeling concept to phenomena that do not involve precisely imitative behavior.

Modeling, theoretically, is seen as encompassing four classes of subprocesses. The first of these are *attentional processes,* which are concerned with questions about what and to what degree various cues from the model register upon the observer. That a person who has a history of rewards for imitation is more likely to imitate may be partly a function of learning to discriminate the cues in a model, which, if followed, will result in reward. Other variables relating to attention are the physical properties of model stimuli (intensity, size, vividness, and novelty, for example); the characteristics of the model that elicit attention, such as social status; the characteristics of the observer, such as low self-esteem, which suggest he will pay greater attention; the incentives for attending; and the discriminability of the modeling stimuli, which is affected both by stimuli and observer variables.

The second class of processes affecting modeled behavior are the processes dealing with *retention of cues*. Rehearsal, especially covert rehearsal, falls into this class, as do symbolic coding operations that allow for more efficient memory. A third class is labeled *motoric reproduction processes* and is concerned with the translation of the retained cue into overt behavior. A person may attend and retain the cues depicting the proper sequence of behavior, but he may be unable to perform the behaviors because he cannot accomplish them at his level of ability. Most of us know how to "dunk" a basketball, having seen it done, but few of us are able to do it. Golf is another illustration: long hours on the practice range may be necessary before we can translate the cues from the instructor-model into anything resembling appropriate behavior.

The fourth and final class of modeling subprocesses are *incentive and motivational processes*. In simple terms: We may attend, retain, and be capable but yet not perform if the perceived incentives are not great enough.

The extension of the basic theory, concerned largely with imitation, to a broader range of modeling phenomena was in part a natural outgrowth of attempts to understand the processes involved in imitation. In part, also, it was due to a desire to explore the implications of modeling for the development of truly novel behavior (as opposed to simple mimicry). For example, in Bandura, Ross, and Ross (1963), subjects observed not one but several models. The resulting behavior was not simple mimicry of any one model but various "combinations of elements from the different models." In Bandura and McDonald (1963) and in Bandura and Mischel (1965), the behavior to be "reproduced" was based on "generalized conceptual and behavioral propensities" toward moral or mature actions. The subjects were faced with entirely different situations from those in which the model had been observed, except that the relevant rules were still appropriate. Similar "rule-modeling" as opposed to simple "behavior-modeling" was demonstrated in language acquisition (Bandura and Harris, 1966).

Modeling produces other effects as well as those that can be called learning. *Disinhibition* refers to the increased likelihood of an already available response that is usually inhibited or suppressed. Asking a girl for a date is "an already available response" in the repertoire of most college males, but the response is often partially inhibited by anxiety about failure. If a model were shown exhibiting "girl-asking," the probability of the male viewer doing the same might be increased, especially if the model were successful. *Inhibition*, on the other hand, might occur if the model were slapped in the face; inhibition is indicated by a decreased probability of response.

Another possible effect of modeling is to elicit a response, either similar to the model's or not. Like disinhibition, *eliciting* increases the probability of a response, but the elicited response had not been inhibited previously. For example, if one had previously been a good golfer but had not played in years, playing with a practiced model might bring forth statements such as, "Oh, yes, now I remember, the ball one inch from the left heel." The "regained" behavior appears more quickly than if the person were to play his comeback game alone.

EFFECTS OF REINFORCEMENT AND PUNISHMENT

A reinforcer is, for most purposes, the same as a reward. A *positive reinforcer* is one that, if presented following a response, will result in increased frequency of responding. A *negative reinforcer* will have a similar effect if it is *removed* following a response. Negative reinforcers that are *presented* following a response are usually called punishments. In general, we are speaking here of consequences, the resulting state of affairs after a response has been made.

Although there is considerable overlap in function between modeling and reinforcement processes, the primary effect of modeling in the theory is to elicit the response, and the primary effect of reinforcers is to strengthen, weaken, or inhibit this response. Bandura and Walters discuss two basic types of reinforcement, which we may call "external" and "internal." External reinforcers are administered by the environment or by some social agent other than oneself. Internal reinforcers, administered by oneself, generally come under the label of *self control mechanisms.*

EXTERNAL REINFORCERS

The treatment of external reinforcers in the theory is exceptional mainly in its extension of traditional learning-theory concepts to the realm of social behavior. For example, the most common pattern of reinforcement used in laboratory studies is "one reward for each correct response." Such a pattern is undoubtedly infrequent in typical social intercourse. Variable patterns—in which sometimes one, sometimes four, and sometimes twenty responses are made before a reward comes—are almost inevitable because of the uncertain presence of reinforcing agents. Interval schedules in which reinforcement comes at certain time intervals are common—for example, when there is a relatively fixed time set aside by a mother for feeding her children.

Very complex patterns of reinforcement, if analyzed, can often be seen as the source of "problem" behaviors. Bandura and Walters give the example of a child seeking attention. Behavior designed to gain this reward occurs with fair frequency, but ordinarily the busy mother responds with interest only at certain intervals. If, however, attention-seeking becomes very frequent or extremely intense, the mother may reward the child with her attention sooner. The result of such a schedule might well be a problem child, one who has learned to perform frequent and intense responses such as tantrums or breaking windows in order to get attention.

On a more theoretical level, Bandura and Walters carefully review laboratory and field studies of the effect of reinforcement and punishment on dependency, sexual behavior, and aggression. The results of such reviews are often critical of time-honored notions in personality theory. An example of a time-honored notion under attack is the frustration-aggression hypothesis, which asserts that frustration inevitably precedes aggression and that aggression is the dominant unlearned response to frustration.

The bulk of the research data indicates that frustration, or the withholding of positive reinforcement, is associated with an increase in motivation, which may be reflected in a temporary intensification of a response. However, the nature of the response to frustration will depend on the prior social training of the frustrated subject, or, more specifically, on the reinforcement and modeling procedures which he has previously experienced. Thus, . . . one can readily produce a highly aggressive child by merely exposing him to successful aggressive models and rewarding the child intermittently for aggressive behavior, while keeping frustration at a very low level (Bandura & Walters, 1963, p. 159).

Bandura and Walters are quick to point out, however, that frustration seems to increase the "vigor" of a response, whatever the response might be, and that responses of high intensity are more likely to be classified as aggressive.

The effect of external reinforcement is most critically examined in conjunction with modeling. The consequences of a response made by a model will have an effect upon the observer, a point we have already discussed in the section on modeling. To amplify those statements, we can say that, generally, observation of a rewarded or punished model produces essentially the same behavioral results as if the response and consequences were the observer's own (Bandura, 1969). Bandura has suggested several explanations of this phenomenon. One is that modeling provides information about the reinforcement contingencies in the environment. The observer knows, in other words, which response is likely to be rewarded and which likely to be punished and will usually act accordingly. Two other interpretations suggested by Bandura do not differ radically from the reinforcement-contingency explanation except that they cause researchers to look at slightly different aspects of the modeling situation. One, suggesting information about "controlling environmental stimuli," deals with those situations in which there is no question about *whether* a response is rewarded or punished but only questions of *when* or *where*. The second suggests that incentives presented to the model may have motivating effects on the observer if the observer is in a state of desire for that particular reward. A response rewarded by food for the model would convey the same reinforcement contingency to any observer; but if an observer were hungry it would probably lead to eager anticipation of a similar reward for himself and, in turn, to faster, more intense, or more persistent matching behavior.

A final interpretation is based on the observation of emotional expressions in the model. Bandura and his associates, in a series of experiments, were able to demonstrate that models' expressive cues associated with pleasure or pain elicit corresponding emotional responses in the observers. Watching a model being shocked and expressing pain or fear, for example, caused definite emotional responses in observers. These responses were measured by physiological recording devices. Moreover, the emotional responses in the observers became conditioned to the stimulus presented to the model, a case of "no-trial" learning (Bandura, 1965). Such emotional responses undoubtedly underlie matching behavior in certain cases.

The four interpretations of response-consequence effects in modeling are not of an "either-or" type. Rather, they represent an attempt to analyze a process into components, any or all of which may be appropriate to a given situation. The explanations are not abstract but highly heuristic; they give clear indications of appropriate research necessary for their confirmation and illumination. This analytic process is characteristic of the Bandura-Walters approach.

INTERNAL REINFORCERS

Reinforcers administered by external social agents, in the long run, are neither a desirable nor a common means of sustaining socially acceptable behavior. Parents are not present all the time. Thus, *self-reward* and *self-punishment* become events of great concern to the personologist. Indeed, once these *self-control mechanisms* are established, the self-evaluations may compete with and prevail over the externally generated response consequences. In any case, in mature children and adults both the internal self-generated stimuli, pleasant or aversive, and the external consequences must be considered in predicting the probable sequence of behavior.

The behavioral phenomena under study here are those that have led to constructs such as self-concept, superego, guilt, shame, and fear. The most direct manifestation of an internal reinforcer occurs when a person refrains from behaving in prohibited ways or when he chooses to behave in a socially acceptable manner, both in the absence of an external agent of reinforcement.

The acquisition of self-control can be seen in studies of modeling and direct reinforcement. Ross (1962), for example, had children play the roles of buyer and salesman in a toy store. When they finished, they were told they could select one and only one toy for their own. If the child-confederate (the model) violated this prohibition by taking three toys, the child-subjects were more likely to do the same. (Subjects were alone in the experimental room when they made their choices.) Children who had observed a model conforming to the prohibition did not conform more than a no-model control group, but they did exhibit significantly less conflict behavior (self-reassurances about deviation, self-directed hostility, and so forth).

Directly studying the determinants of self-reward and self-evaluative responses, Bandura and Kupers (1963) used child subjects in a bowling game. In one condition, the model would not take "free" candy unless he had achieved a high score. In another, the model administered self-reward with a much lower standard of performance (score). In the absence of models, the children bowled and helped themselves to candy as they wished. It was found that their standards of self-reward closely matched those of their particular model.

Direct reinforcement of socially acceptable behaviors or punishment of anti-social acts can also induce self-control. Punishment, in particular, has been the object of a number of studies in which the *timing* of the punishment has been varied. Broadly, the results suggest that punishment is most effective in reducing undesirable behavior if it *precedes* the response (Aronfreed and Reber, 1965). Punishment following the response seems more likely to result in "guilt" (association of unpleasant stimuli with the completion of an act) than in response decrease. Since most parents who use punishment in child training administer the "whip" following the response, we could expect to find less effective behavior control than with parents using rewarding methods— a quite general finding in developmental research.

TECHNIQUES FOR BEHAVIOR MODIFICATION

With their professed goal of discovering the determinants of human behavior, it was logical that Bandura and Walters would eventually investigate techniques for modifying behavior. If one has discovered a determinant of behavior, then one should be able to vary the behavior by varying the determinant. Predictable behavior modification is, in part, a test of the hypothesized relationship between the determinant and its effect. In part, also, behavior modification is applied science. Child training and psychotherapy, for example, are disciplines which are based upon techniques for behavior control and change; principles developed in research should be applicable in these disciplines. Bandura and Walters discuss five techniques they feel are immediately useful.

The first of these is *extinction*. The "problem behavior" to which this technique is applicable is that behavior which is deemed undesirable. In some cases in which the behavior is frequent because of positive reinforcement, it can be reduced or eliminated simply by withdrawing the reinforcer. Williams (1959) describes the case of a young boy with strong dependency habits, such as crying and demanding his parents' extended presence at bedtime. The reinforcement in this case was the parents' response—going to him at night and comforting him. In order to get the boy to sleep, the parents withdrew the reinforcer, that is, they put the boy to bed (with loving attention), then closed the door and ignored all crying, no matter how long and how loud. The first night the child cried almost an hour. The second night was much better, and by the end of a week the child no longer cried when left in his room but instead played happily until he dropped off to sleep.

In behaviors that are maintained by the reduction of fear or anxiety, extinction is more difficult. For example, in a case treated by Herzberg (1941), a woman was afraid to go out of the house alone. It was impossible to remove the fear-producing stimulus, whatever it was, because the woman refused to leave the house. The phobic behavior was reinforced by the reduction of fear; the behavior was being maintained and strengthened even though a test (going outside) would have shown the fear to be groundless. The therapist had to force the woman to undergo a graduated series of tests in order to extinguish the behavior. He had her walk in a park first, which was less anxiety-provoking than walking in a crowded street, then in a quiet street, and then finally in a crowded street. Eventually she was able to walk in streets without experiencing any fear or psychosomatic reactions.

The second technique of behavior modification is *counterconditioning*, eliciting responses that are incompatible with the undesirable behavior. Wolpe (1958) had his patients practice relaxation (the incompatible response), then asked them while they relaxed to imagine scenes that were anxiety-provoking for them. As is usually the case in anxiety reactions, this procedure worked best if the patient began with an imagined situation that was only mildly frightening and worked up to more intense scenes. The goal of this technique is to neutralize the anxiety-provoking stimuli by pairing them with positive experiences.

Counterconditioning also can be applied to behaviors that are not anxiety-provoking. For example, a not uncommon treatment of sexual perversion is the association of the deviant behavior with induced noxious stimuli such as shock or nausea. Raymond (1956) had a patient overcome his fetish for women's handbags by presenting him with a collection of handbags while causing him to experience chemically induced nausea. Similar treatment is often used with alcoholics.

In cases in which a person's problems stem from the fact that he lacks appropriate behavior for coping with the environment, *positive reinforcement* is often effective. For example, to increase social responsiveness, often lacking in withdrawn schizophrenics, King, Armitage, and Tilton (1960) rewarded communication and cooperation with therapists and other patients. Other types of behavior deficit for which this technique is seen as appropriate include autistic children (rewarding social communication) and criminals (rewarding prosocial behavior).

The fourth behavior-modification technique is *modeling*. As one would gather from their research, Bandura and Walters consider this a highly useful and effective technique for eliciting desirable behaviors not present in the person's repertoire. Once the behavior is elicited, other means, such as positive reinforcement, can be applied to strengthen and maintain it. For example, a model that exhibits desirable social behavior can elicit the same desirable responses in others.

The modeling process can also be effective in overcoming fears and inhibitions and the resulting avoidance behaviors, as in an experiment which significantly reduced phobic behavior (fearful avoidance) of children toward dogs by exposing them to a fearless child model interacting with a friendly dog (Bandura, Grusec, and Menlove, 1967).

Modeling has several other advantages as a therapeutic technique. For one, the behavior to be imitated can be presented on film: complex behaviors are seen as a whole in a relatively inexpensive medium and in a short time. The film can be shown to a large group; patients need not be treated individually. On film or not, the situation depicted may include the consequences of the behavior and thus lead to vicarious learning. Modeling can be used to extinguish undesirable antisocial behavior (bad consequences) as well as fears and inhibitions (no "injuring" consequences).

The fifth and final technique discussed by Bandura and Walters is *discrimination learning*. Such learning occurs, as its label implies, when one learns to respond to one stimulus but not to another, similar stimulus. Often the process involves first learning a response to one stimulus, *generalizing* it to the second stimulus, and then extinguishing the unnecessary, unproductive, or undesirable response to the second stimulus. A child, for example, may generalize habits learned with reference to his father to other male authority figures such as teachers and policemen. He must learn that not all the responses appropriate to his father are similarly appropriate to these other figures.

To produce discrimination learning one follows the basic procedure described above: reward the response to the desirable stimulus and punish (or not reward) the response to the inappropriate stimulus. Freund (1960) has treated homosexuals in this manner by administering noxious stimuli while the homosexual viewed pictures of nude males and then administering pleasant stimuli while he viewed pictures of nude females.

THE SOCIAL LEARNING VIEW OF MAN

Every personality theory, in the way it proceeds, has a view of man as a human being. Carl Rogers views man as something with an innate drive to better (actualize) himself; Rogers' therapy is intended to remove obstacles to such personal growth. In contrast, the social learning approach takes a very active role in therapy, with carefully planned and deliberate interventions in the learning history of the individual. For this reason, the approach is sometimes scorned as "manipulative" or, more generally, "inhuman." This is an issue, partly empirical, partly philosophical, that will certainly not be decided in the pages of this brief book. But, in fairness, we will present the view of man in the social learning approach as the approach's advocates see it. Contrary to some opinions, Bandura and Walters are not inhuman.

First, the social learning theorists suggest that the "inhuman" label is wrongly placed on them and that it more deservedly belongs on those who practice ineffective therapy. Is it human, they ask, to refuse help to a person in need when help is available? Take the example of an autistic child who frequently engages in bizarre self-stimulatory behavior. In any therapy, the therapist must have the attention of the patient, attention that is denied during these self-stimulatory episodes. Lovaas (1966), a social learning therapist, is not unwilling to use firm techniques to stop the self-stimulation and regain attention. A sharp slap on the thigh achieves its effect, and progress toward a fulfilling life continues. Lovaas has been called cruel and, of course, inhuman for such interventions, but is it really more human to passively let the patient continue in inappropriate behavior? Suppose that, instead of being self-stimulatory, the behavior were self-destructive, such as banging the head on a table. To do nothing or to merely alleviate the harmful effects (temporarily) by padding the table might be less subject to complaints of manipulation, but the active extinction and elimination of the self-destructive behavior is certainly more human in the long run.

Stated more positively, the social learning approach views man as someone whose behavior results from continual reciprocal interaction between himself and the environment. The environment clearly exerts control over man, but man also controls—often to a highly significant extent—the environment. Not only may man choose his environment, but also man's behavior can modify his environment once chosen. Without choice, animals in an experiment by Sidman (1966) were placed in an aversive environment, one with shocks. If the animal pressed a lever, however, the shocks did not come; the effect of the animal's behavior was to create a nonaversive environment. In like manner, much of the environment of man is of man's own making. Raush (1965) has shown that aggressive children, through their actions, often create a hostile environment, while friendly children often create a generally friendly world. In fact, if it were not true that each person partially creates his environment, social learning therapy would be much less useful: once out in his natural environment, the patient would have many of his newly formed behaviors extinguished or rendered ineffective.

Much of the controversy over control versus freedom, too, has to do with objectives—what the therapist hopes to attain for his patient. These objectives are often highly value-laden. Bandura (1969) makes the interesting point that it is at this juncture that the question of ethics becomes most urgent. He asserts that it is the client's right to decide on the objectives and that abrogation of this right, in any therapeutic or controlling process, justly deserves the label "manipulation." A medical doctor is ethical if a patient asks to be relieved of anxiety and a tranquilizer is deemed medically appropriate. Were the doctor to decide on his own that nobody likes anxiety and thereupon dump a ton of tranquilizer in the city's reservoir, his ethical judgment would be suspect.

Finally, the development of certain behaviors through active intervention may actually increase the freedom of the individual. Self-restraint reduces freedom if there is no good reason for restraint, as in abnormal phobias and fears; it may, on the other hand, increase freedom if it prevents behaviors that are subject to strong societal sanctions, such as criminal acts. Training in the alleviation of rigid self-restraining processes, in the first case, and in their establishment, in the second, would free the individual for more productive and fulfilling human activities. In general, the development of effective self-regulatory processes is likely to produce behaviors and environments that represent true personal growth. The conflict between behavioral approaches and humanistic morality, according to Bandura, is only an apparent conflict, and it is highly misleading to assume that it is real.

SUMMARY

The social learning theory of Bandura and Walters has a view of man, represents an approach to the study of personality, and is the basis of applied procedures in child training and psychotherapy. It began and continues as a theory aimed toward experimentation; the empirical output of Bandura and Walters alone is staggering, not to mention the many other researchers of like mind working on similar problems. It has a cookbook flavor, both in its specifications of research possibilities and in its techniques for behavior modification. If "cookbook" means a systematic, organized way of proceeding, no doubt Bandura and Walters would accept the label.

One of the most important contributions of the theory-related research is the concept of modeling. The use of modeling in behavior modification, in the development of novel acts, in the analysis of subprocesses, in establishing self-controlling mechanisms—all are invaluable additions to general personology and clearly form the characteristic base for the Bandura-Walters approach. Modeling involves learning, albeit vicarious or observational learning. It is affected by motivation and reinforcement in ways analogous to direct learning processes. And it is profoundly social, both in that two or more people are usually present and in that it deals with situations occurring frequently in everyday life.

The increasingly frequent appearance of learning theory approaches to personality has excited many scientists, and therapists as well. Researchers in personality have responded to the clear dimensional variables in the theory and, having often despaired of doubtfully valid personality tests and of the ubiquitous correlational studies, are happily working with behavior. Therapists who have longed for a more active role and more clearly defined results are applying many of the experimental techniques in institutional settings, an event that promises benefits to both institution and theory. Like all theories, however, the Bandura-Walters approach has a certain range of phenomena to which it is particularly suited. The future holds many problems, many hours of experimentation, then theory revisions and more experimentation as the theory is developed to deal more directly with complex personal and social problems. The ultimate usefulness of the approach, and of others like it, is an empirical question, a status clearly acceptable to Bandura and Walters.

REFERENCES

Aronfreed, J., & Reber, A. Internalized behavioral suppression and the timing of social punishment. *Journal of Personality and Social Psychology*, 1965, 1, 3–16.

Bandura, A. Vicarious processes: A case of no-trial learning. In L. Berkowitz (Ed.), *Advances in experimental social psychology*. Vol. II. New York: Academic Press, 1965.

Bandura, A. *Principles of behavioral modification*. New York: Holt, Rinehart and Winston, 1969.

Bandura, A., Grusec, J. E., & Menlove, F. L. Vicarious extinction of avoidance behavior. *Journal of Personality and Social Psychology*, 1967, **5**, 16–23.

Bandura, A., & Harris, M. B. Modification of syntactic style. *Journal of Experimental Child Psychology*, 1966, **4**, 341–352.

Bandura, A., & Kupers, C. J. Transmission of patterns of self-reinforcement through modeling. *Journal of Abnormal and Social Psychology*, 1964, **69**, 1–9.

Bandura, A., & McDonald, F. J. Influence of social reinforcement and the behavior of models in shaping children's moral judgments. *Journal of Abnormal and Social Psychology*, 1963, **67**, 274–281.

Bandura, A., & Mischel, W. Modification of self-imposed delay of reward through exposure to live and symbolic models. *Journal of Personality and Social Psychology*, 1965, **2**, 698–705.

Bandura, A., Ross, D., & Ross, S. A. Transmission of aggression through imitation of aggressive models. *Journal of Abnormal and Social Psychology*, 1961, **63**, 575–582.

Bandura, A., Ross, D., & Ross, S. A. A comparative test of the status envy, social power, and secondary reinforcement theories of identificatory learning. *Journal of Abnormal and Social Psychology*, 1963, **67**, 527–534.

Bandura, A., & Walters, R. H. *Adolescent aggression*. New York: Ronald Press, 1959.

Bandura, A., & Walters, R. H. *Social learning and personality development*. New York: Holt, Rinehart and Winston, 1963.

Freund, K. Some problems in the treatment of homosexuality. In H. J. Eysenck (Ed.), *Behavior therapy and the neuroses*. New York: Pergamon, 1960.

Herzberg, A. Short treatment of neuroses by graduated tasks. *British Journal of Medical Psychology*, 1941, **19**, 36–51.

King, G. F., Armitage, S. G., & Tilton, J. R. A therapeutic approach to schizophrenics of extreme pathology. *Journal of Abnormal and Social Psychology*, 1960, **61**, 276–286.

Lovaas, O. I. *Reinforcement therapy* (16 mm. sound film). Philadelphia: Smith, Kline & French Laboratories, 1966.

Raush, H. L. Interaction sequences. *Journal of Personality and Social Psychology*, 1965, **2**, 487–499.

Raymond, M. S. Case of fetishism treated by aversion therapy. *British Medical Journal*, 1956, **2**, 854–856.

Ross, S. A. The effect of deviant and nondeviant models on the behavior of preschool children. Unpublished doctoral dissertation, Stanford University, 1962.

Sidman, M. Avoidance behavior. In W. K. Honig (Ed.), *Operant behavior*. New York: Appleton-Century-Crofts, 1966.

Skinner, B. F. *Science and human behavior.* New York: Macmillan, 1953.

Williams, C. D. The elimination of tantrum behavior by extinction procedures. *Journal of Abnormal and Social Psychology,* 1959, **59**, 269.

Wolpe, J. *Psychotherapy by reciprocal inhibition.* Stanford, Calif.: Stanford Univ. Press, 1958.

Rogers' theory of personality has developed from a therapeutic technique that is variously described as "nondirective" or "client-centered." The implication of these terms is that the person (patient or client) has within him the ability and motivation to improve himself and that the therapist's role is primarily one of facilitating that improvement. The theory is "humanistic" and hence, more than most theories, is compatible with common religious beliefs; it fits, too, in our everyday language system, which is marked by terms like "free will," choice, and personal responsibility. Such an approach to human behavior generally leads to an emphasis on the "self" and the characteristics of the self, and Rogers' theory is no exception. In addition, the approach will have a flavor of observation rather than intervention. Instead of using experimental phrasing such as "If I do this to him, then . . . ," Rogers thinks this way:

> If certain conditions exist . . . , then a process will occur. . . . If this process . . . occurs, then certain personality and behavioral changes . . . will occur (1959, p. 212).

THERAPEUTIC BASIS OF ROGERS' THEORY

Rogers' view of human nature and of the conditions necessary for behavior change evolved slowly from a purely applied attempt to help patients. The personality theory, if indeed it can be viewed separately, is strongly anchored in Rogers' view of how therapy proceeds, and therefore we must consider this "theory of therapy" in order to understand the "theory of personality."

Following the conditions-process-outcome format of Rogers' thinking, the necessary conditions, if therapy is to occur, are these: The client presents himself in a state of *incongruence,* which means there is some discrepancy between the way he perceives himself (his *self*) and what he is experiencing. The person may perceive himself as a friendly, likeable person, for example, but yet find only open expressions of hostility and rejection from other people. Such incongruence, which need not be conscious, makes the person vulnerable to anxiety, depression, and threat, in the sense of a threatened self-image. The anxiety and threat, may lead to maladaptive and defensive distortions of his experiences. The therapist, if he is to help the patient, must be congruent and must experience *unconditional positive regard* toward the client and *empathetic understanding* of the client's subjective thoughts and feeling. *Congruent* here means that the therapist does not distort what is happening between himself and the client. *Unconditional positive regard* refers to a distinction between the person and the person's behaviors and expressed thoughts: the person is always of great value (positively regarded) no matter what the therapist thinks of specific acts or feelings. *Empathy* means to perceive accurately what the client is thinking and feeling. The final condition for therapy is that the client "at least to a minimal degree" perceive the unconditional positive regard and the empathy of the therapist.

If these conditions exist, a process occurs. The patient, with increasing frequency, begins to express his feelings openly. These expressions usually relate to the *self* and to the relationship between self and experience. Through them, the incongruence between self and experience is articulated and resolved by a reorganization of the self-structure.

Note how the process depends upon the conditions. The unconditional positive regard, in particular, on the part of the therapist enables the client to express his feelings openly so that natural processes can work. The therapist's empathy and congruence enable him to perceive accurately the thoughts and feelings of the client and hence make it possible for him to aid in the process of articulation. Note also, however, the emphasis on the patient "doing it by himself" (client-centered, nondirective). Rogers assumes that humans have an "inherent tendency . . . to develop all . . . capacities in ways which serve to maintain or enhance" the person (1959, p. 196). This *actualizing tendency*, in reference to the self (*self-actualization*), means essentially a striving toward congruence between self and experience. The person, indeed, would obtain congruence on his own were it not for the denials and distortions of experience caused by the threat to self-image and the anxiety produced by incongruence. This is the job of the therapist, in Rogers' view: to make these distortions unnecessary through continuing unconditional positive regard.

The outcome of the therapeutic process is indicated by the process itself. The client becomes more congruent, less defensive, and less anxious. His perception of himself and his experience becomes more accurate. He is more confident, indeed, more capable, and he experiences more *positive self-regard*. His *ideal self*, that "self" on which he places the highest value, becomes more realistic; his "real" self and his ideal self become more congruent. In short, the client would be described by an outside observer as more mature and better adjusted.

ROGERS' THEORY OF PERSONALITY

Perhaps the most important construct in Rogers' theory of personality is that of *self*. As is apparent from the discussion of therapy, this
concept is almost indispensable to Rogers when he speaks of human
behavior. It was not always so: "I began my work," says Rogers (1959,
p. 200), "with the settled notion that the 'self' was a vague, ambiguous,
scientifically meaningless term which had gone out of the psychologist's vocabulary with the departure of the introspectionists." Unfortunately, Rogers' patients insisted on using the term, and slowly he
realized that "in some odd sense . . . [the client's] goal was to become
his 'real self'" (1959, p. 201).

Despite the increasing importance of self, its definition remained
somewhat vague, and acceptable observable criteria for the construct
were unavailable. Attitudes toward self, however, could be studied, and
Rogers did so, observing attitudinal changes in therapy. Attitudes did
change in a positive direction, as predicted.

At the same time, clinical experience was sharpening Rogers' notion of the self. The client's perception of self changed so quickly at
times that Rogers was led to view the self as a gestalt or configuration
which could be radically altered by some change rather than as a
stable entity. Another notable development was the incorporation of the
consistency notion: the notion that the self is a configuration that
endeavors to accept facts consistent with the already existing pattern
and to reject facts that are not consistent. The corollary construct of
congruence was thereby born.

Stephenson (1953) developed a procedure called the Q technique
which promised to create an acceptable observable criterion for the
self construct. In essence, the Q technique has the subject (client)
consider a set of self-referent statements or adjectives and place them
into categories ranging from, say "most characteristic of me" to "least
characteristic of me." Examples of such statements, from Nunnally
(1955), are "I am calm and placid most of the time," and "I am very
self-conscious about sex." The subject is forced to place a certain number of statements into each category, so that the final distribution allows
a fairly elaborate statistical treatment.

The methodological advance represented by the Q technique illuminated another issue. The sorting task could be (and was) performed
for all types of selves. For example (Nunnally, 1955), a subject would
form one distribution under an instruction to describe himself "as I am
generally," that is, the "self" as Rogers usually uses the term. The subject would then form a second distribution under an instruction to
describe himself "as I would like to be" (the ideal self), and so on for
a large number of additional selves: "as I was from 9 to 16 years of

age," "as I think I am becoming," "as my friends regard me," and so forth. These many selves are in the process of theoretical organization in Rogers' theory, but we shall be mostly concerned with the "real" and the ideal selves.

Rogers' theory of personality introduces no constructs which have not been used in his understanding of the therapeutic process; rather, the constructs are an extension of these ideas to the format of a general theory of personality. The underlying assumption, which provides the basic motivational key to the theory, is that of a tendency toward self-actualization. "Behavior is the goal-directed attempt of the organism to satisfy the experienced needs for actualization in the reality as perceived" (1959, p. 222). Similar statements are made about behavior and about the value a person places on experiences. That which is "perceived as maintaining or enhancing the organism" is valued positively; in gross terms, a person will approach actualizing experiences and avoid those not so perceived.

The self develops when parts of the person's conscious awareness become associated with feelings of "belongingness." Especially included are awareness of *being* and awareness of *function* (what "I" am and what "I" can do). Almost as a corollary of the fundamental axiom of actualization, there develops with the self a need for *positive regard* both by self and by others. When other people with whom the person interacts come to see certain thoughts and behaviors as more or less worthy of regard, the person takes this as *conditional* positive regard of self; the self becomes selective in thought and behavior so as to satisfy these "conditions."

Two systems have now developed, both of which determine behavior. The one, based on self-actualization, approaches or avoids depending on whether or not the resulting experience is seen as one which will enhance the person. The other, based on the need for positive regard, approaches or avoids depending on whether or not the resulting experience is seen as one which will meet with approval from significant others (or from the self, when the viewpoint of others has been internalized). Needless to say, the person often encounters situations in which one basic need says "approach" while the other says "avoid." Learning a new skill, for example, often means embarrassment in the early, awkward stages but, when accomplished, adds to the competence of the individual. It is within the conflict of these two basic needs, the need for actualization and the need for positive regard, that the trauma of individual history is enacted. Advance and relapse, adjustment and maladjustment—all can be traced to the working out of an individual solution to this conflict.

To the extent that the need for positive regard dictates choice over the need for actualization, incongruence between self and experience will develop. In Rogers' words, the person

has not been true to himself, to his own natural optimistic valuing of experience, but for the sake of preserving the positive regard of others has now come to falsify some of the values he experiences and to perceive them only in terms based upon their value to others (1959, p. 226).

With the incongruence come vulnerability to threat and anxiety, and defensive distortion of one's experiences. When the incongruence reaches too high a level the person will seek help, or be forced to seek help, from an institution created for such a purpose or from a psychologist, psychiatrist, priest, educational counselor, etc.

Individual personality is characterized in Rogers' theory both by the content of the self-concept (as in Q technique) and by positions on the various dimensional constructs we have mentioned. Because of their previous experiences, particularly with parents and with reference to their culture, persons vary in the degree to which the need for positive regard requires that thought and behavior be evaluated in ways not in accord with their potential actualizing value. In other words, the need for positive regard does not necessarily conflict with the need for actualizing. If parents consistently exhibit unconditional positive regard, the self-regard will likely be unconditional also. This does not mean that parents or self see all actions as equally desirable but rather that a distinction is made between the person and his behaviors. Many religions avow the wisdom of this principle by insisting on the immutable value of the man no matter how heinous his behavior.

Self-regard itself is a topic of concern to the theory and has generated considerable research. A person with high self-esteem, for example, tends to be well adjusted and more competent both in interpersonal relations and in achievement tasks. A brief but informative introduction to such research can be found in Dreger, 1962, pp. 153–156.

In fact, it is somewhat surprising to note the many possibilities for research on Rogers' theory, given the mystical tone of its constructs. It is a tribute to a fine mind that this is the case, of course, and to Rogers' continual efforts to create workable scientific constructs without destroying the distinctive humanity of his theory.

There is another aspect of Rogers' "humanistic" nomenclature that is worth considering. The constructs of the theory are closely associated with the implicit theories of the individual (clients) themselves —that is, they are "in" the same language system of freedom and responsibility. The constructs also place heavy stress on individual effort (do it yourself). The result of this is to make the theory compatible with other social systems, such as the religious and legal systems, to name two. On the level of the individual, the theory tends to phrase problems in a language system that the client can understand because he uses it in his everyday life. For example, some theories point to an event in the client's past and say, in effect, "That is why you are what you are now." It is a psychological commonplace to say some such thing as, "'You grew up in a slum, so therefore you are anxious today." The client often can accept and understand such a deterministic explanation, but it gives him no basis for future action: "O.K., what do I do now?"

Rogers' theory, on the other hand, places full responsibility upon the individual. It says, "You have within you the power to change your life. It's up to you to do so. Not me, the therapist, and not the environment. You." In Rogers' words:

We have frequently observed that when the individual has been authoritatively told that he is governed by certain factors or conditions beyond his control, it makes therapy more difficult, and it is only when the individual discovers for himself that he can organize his perceptions that change is possible. In veterans who have been given their own psychiatric diagnosis, the effect is often that of making the individual feel that he is under an unalterable doom, that he is unable to control the organization of his life. When, however, the self sees itself as capable of reorganizing its own perceptual field, a marked change in basic confidence occurs. . . . A veteran at the conclusion of counseling puts it more briefly and more positively: "My attitude toward myself is changed now to where I feel I *can* do something with my self and my life." He has come to view himself as the instrument by which some reorganization can take place (1947, pp. 361–362).

SUMMARY

Rogers' theory defies easy classification. It does reflect a somewhat greater perceptual-cognitive emphasis than those theories that have preceded it in this book. This perceptual-cognitive functioning is never systematically clarified, it is something that is more or less assumed to be happening within the person. The person has a "view" of reality and a notion of what he thinks reality should be like. Discrepancy between these views constitutes incongruence, but the actual content of the views is rarely considered in the theory.

An extremely general conceptualization of two basic needs—for actualization and a need for positive regard—encompasses all significant human behavior. Since these constructs are so general, they are extremely difficult to find observable criteria for. Rogers does not seem to mind, as long as there is some meaning for a given individual. The therapist's task, after all, is not to intervene but to present a situation of love, honesty, and openness. Within such a situation, the best of human motivations can fulfill themselves.

The "human" flavor of the theory has resulted in Rogers' current status among the more romantic techniques gaining prominence in psychotherapy. Encounter groups, sensitivity training groups, and generally "existential" methods of treatment often count Rogers and others of similar persuasion (for example, Maslow) as "heroes."

Rogers' contribution to research is significant. His concepts of self and congruence, in particular, have been exceptionally heuristic. Some personologists have rightly criticized this research for its lack of attention to changes in behavior while it studies changes in attitudes and self-concept. But attitude studies in general find themselves subject to such criticisms, and in any case, the fault lies in the experimentation more than in the theory itself.

REFERENCES

Dreger, R. M. *Fundamentals of personality.* Philadelphia: Lippincott, 1962.

Nunnally, J. C. An investigation of some propositions of self-conception. *Journal of Abnormal and Social Psychology,* 1955, **50**, 87–92.

Rogers, C. R. *Counseling and psychotherapy.* Boston: Houghton Mifflin, 1942.

Rogers, C. R. Some observations on the organization of personality. *American Psychologist,* 1947, **2**, 358–368.

Rogers, C. R. *Client-centered therapy.* Boston: Houghton Mifflin, 1951.

Rogers, C. R. A theory of therapy, personality, and interpersonal relationships. In S. Koch (Ed.), *Psychology: a study of a science.* Vol. III. New York: McGraw-Hill, 1959.

Rogers, C. R. *On becoming a person.* Boston: Houghton Mifflin, 1961.

Rogers, C. R., & Dymond, R. F. (Eds.). *Psychotherapy and personality change.* Chicago: Univ. Chicago Press, 1954.

Stephenson, W. *The study of behavior.* Chicago: Univ. Chicago Press, 1953.

Kurt Lewin and his theory are mysteries in many respects. The writings that contain the man and his thought are not well organized; they often represent his ideas on a particular issue, practical or theoretical, rather than on the theory as a whole. Any semi-organized description, such as we will attempt here, must reorganize the insightful bits and pieces from wherever they appear. Almost always we find a sigh and a warning from his Boswells, such as Deutsch (1954, p. 189): "It is well to realize at the outset that Lewin's theoretical system was never fully developed nor was it formalized into a hypothetico-deductive system."

Once the outline of his basic theory is recognized, however, one is often stunned by its simplicity. This impression then gives way to exasperation as the vagueness of some of the concepts obstructs effective use. Finally, realization that the vagueness was intentional and an understanding of the metatheoretical complexity of the simple constructs bring a glimpse of why Lewin was (and remains) one of the most important figures not only in personology but also in social psychology.

Lewin's theory of personality is commonly classified as "field theory," a concept already encountered in Murphy (see Chapter 3). Field theory refers to an approach in which behavior is seen as something that occurs in a field or organized system. This system may be conceptualized as having various parts, such as "person" and "environment," but there is a reluctance to identify the behavior with either component exclusively. $B = f(P,E)$. Behavior is a function of the Person *and* the Environment.

Lewin was also prone to use constructs taken from mathematics and from field theories in the physical sciences. In a sense, his theory is one of the first mathematical models in psychology. Because of the imperfect analogies between physical and psychological constructs and because of the necessary vagueness in the latter, however, mathematical predictions and considerations have played only a very small role in the use of the theory. But it is worth noting Lewin's intention in order to understand why the concepts took the form they did. The particular branch of mathematics concerned here is topology, which deals with spatial relationships; hence you will sometimes find the theory referred to as "topological." It is also sometimes called a "vector psychology" after one of its most prominent theoretical constructs. The main divisions of the *field* in which behavior occurs are *person* and *environment*, with environment further differentiated into psychological and nonpsychological parts. The person and his psychological environment constitute the *life space*, and in this theoretical "space" we attempt to understand the person's behavior. Such a formulation says little more than that the person and what the person *perceives* to be the situation (his psychological environment) will jointly determine his response. $B = f(P, E)$.

Within the psychological environment there are various areas designated *regions* that correspond with dynamic aspects of the situation. If, for example, a person is faced with a choice between studying or going to a movie, the environment would contain (at least) two regions roughly corresponding to these decision alternatives. One should not be misled into taking the spatial analogy literally, however; a girl who has been unexpectedly kissed by a boy may have two dynamic regions corresponding to "returning the kiss" and "slapping his face," both of which are spatially located in the general vicinity of the boy's head.

Behavior begins in the life space when a *need* is aroused in a person. Needs may result from physiological arousal (for example, hunger) or they may represent any desire, hope, or even "intention" of the individual. Partly because of the needs active at a given time, certain regions of the psychological environment take on value for a person. *Valence* is Lewin's term for such value, which may vary from high positive to high negative. Also because of needs, certain forces are applied to the person to move toward regions of positive valence or away from those with negative valence. These forces are called *vectors.*

The simple terms *person, psychological environment* with *regions, needs, vector,* and *valence* contain the essentials of Lewin's theory. A need arises in a person and creates valence in environmental regions. The need also causes vector forces on the person to move in his life space toward (or away from) those regions. Such movement, if it occurs, is called *locomotion* and is often reflected in the behavior of the individual. (Locomotion, however, may occur in thought only.) For example, a drink has high positive valence for a thirsty (need) alcoholic; there is a pressure (vector) on him to move (locomote) toward the drink. We have already a nutshell version of the theory; we will now examine in more detail each of these constructs and its role in Lewin's theory and then turn to some applications of the approach to common psychological phenomena.

BASIC CONSTRUCTS

NEED

Need is the most basic of the basic constructs. Needs determine both valence and vector and thereby behavior and thought. It is therefore surprising to find so little explication of need in the theory. As we have mentioned, everything that could be considered as having motivational implications is a "need," from the most primitive urges to the most idiosyncratic intentions. One can have the need to eat and also the need to wind the yellow clock in the guest bedroom before 9:30 p.m. Lewis was perseverant in his refusal to list or classify needs or to speak more definitively about their nature. These are the tasks of experimental investigation, in his opinion; premature systematization of a fundamental construct results only in severe limitations in the scope of any theory based on the construct (1951). Supported by research from Karsten (1928), Lewin did begin to distinguish states of needs in general—undersatiated, satiated, and oversatiated. The degree of satiation determines, in part, the valence of the environmental regions associated with the need. When a person is hungry (undersatiated) food is positive in valence, but if the hungry person overeats (oversatiation) food may become negative in valence. Remember that Thanksgiving dinner? From other research, Lewin allowed that needs can be created by an intention to finish a task. Research on the effects of interrupted tasks is an important area and will be discussed in more detail later.

Need, in Lewin's theory, is an energy construct. It is the starter, the motor, of behavior. It creates *tension* in the person. Here we must point out that the person, one region among many in the life space, is itself divided into several subregions, sometimes called systems or cells. When tension arises, it usually does so in one of these subregions, not in the person as a whole. The goal of behavior or thought is properly to equalize tension in these intrapersonal subregions, even though equalization may consist merely of reducing tension in the aggravated system to the level of the others.

Finally, it should be noted that the relatively ambiguous "field" definition of need has had the entirely beneficial effect of leading psychologists to look more frequently to the social environment for the source of motivation. Rather than use a strictly physiological or intrapersonal approach, Lewin chose to conceive of many "stimulus-induced" needs—needs that arise because of something encountered in the environment. A newspaper headline can induce tension, a need. This focus on the need-inducing aspects of the environment has brought Lewin many followers in social psychology. Festinger (see Chapter 13), for example, was clearly influenced by Lewin.

VALENCE

Valence is a property of a region of the psychological environment. In later works, Lewin thought of a valenced region as a force-field, something that creates a force toward (positive) or away from (negative) the region. Its ultimate source, however, is a need. A region of positive valence is one which, if entered, reduces the tension from the need; at least the individual perceives that the tension will be reduced.

VECTOR

A vector is a psychological force, the direct determinant of thought or behavior. In diagrams, a vector is shown as an arrow implying force and demonstrating three aspects of that force: *direction,* by the direction in which the arrow is pointing; *intensity,* by the length of the arrow; and *point of application.* The point of application is usually on the person as a whole, but, if more detailed analysis is required, it may be on a particular subregion of the person.

To understand the meaning and significance of the three major dynamic concepts in Lewin's theory—need (or tension), vector, and valence—it is helpful to consider all three together. As in most theories, the need-tension is basic, profoundly influencing, if not completely determining, the vector (force) and valence (value). Unlike most theories, however, the effect of needs is indirect. Vectors, generally speaking, are determined by valences. The direction of a vector is either toward a region of positive valence or away from a region of negative valence. The intensity of the vector-force is a function of the intensity of the valence (directly), and of the psychological distance between the person and the valanced region (inversely). Valence, in turn, is largely determined by the satiating potential of the region for the active needs and by the strength of need itself. However, other factors (other than those derived from needs) can influence the strength of valence. Lewin mentions "the character and state of the person" and "the perceived nature of the object or activity" represented in the region (1938). While such designations are good examples of Lewin's intentional vagueness, the reader should be aware that linking need to characteristics of the psychological environment (valence) instead of to behavior directly is a profoundly significant development. Need becomes merely one of several determinants of behavior, in such a way that the other determinants (to be understood through research) can be efficiently integrated with need to produce valence. Even the multi-determined valence does not translate directly into behavior; it must compete with valences of other regions in order to determine the resultant force (vector).

REGIONS

Regions within the psychological environment or within the person are by no means characteristically similar. We have already mentioned *psychological distance*. Regions which are closer to one another, in some psychological sense, exert more mutual influence. To daydream and to study, for example, may be closer than to study and to go to a movie; it is easier to shift from studying to daydreaming than to movie-watching.

A second property of regions is *fluidity-rigidity*. A fluid region is one that responds quickly to influence. A third property is *permeability*, which is an aspect more of a boundary than of a region. If communication or movement between two regions is difficult, then the two regions are said to be relatively impermeable. An impermeable boundary is also called a *barrier*.

Putting all these properties together, we may say that a region that is distant, rigid, and relatively impermeable is not likely to be influenced by the person or by things occurring in other regions.

LOCOMOTION AND COMMUNICATION

Locomotion refers to a change of position, usually of the person, in the life space. Change of position, in turn, usually refers to movement from one region to another. It may involve behavior, or if one stops studying and starts daydreaming, only thought.

Locomotion is to be distinguished from communication, which generally applies to two regions and their mutual influence. Two innerpersonal regions, for example, may "communicate" if an increase in tension in one is accompanied by an increase in the other. If a person believes that killing in any context is wrong and also believes that Americans should not refuse military service, we might say that these two psychological "facts" are *not* in communication with one another.

APPLICATIONS

In order to show Lewin's theory "at work," while concurrently noting a few of the many areas of human behavior for which conceptualization in Lewinian terms has been highly influential, we will look at three applications of the theory: intrapersonal conflict, uncompleted tasks, and level of aspiration.

INTRAPERSONAL CONFLICT

Conflict is defined by Lewin as the state that occurs when two or more opposing forces (vectors) are approximately equal. The more common types are diagrammed in Figure 3 as they have been introduced into the general terminology by Lewin and his associates (see also Miller and Dollard, Chapter 7). *Approach-approach conflict* occurs when the force toward *A* approximates the force to move toward *B*. This type of conflict is easily resolved because force is an inverse function of psychological distance, which we are here representing by spatial distance. Any locomotion toward *A*, for example, will increase the force toward *A* and reduce the force toward *B*, hence resolving the conflict. Such a conflict can be illustrated by a hungry person having to choose between almost equally desirable steak and seafood.

A choice between a painful shock and a hit on the head is not so easily resolved. This type of conflict, choosing between two undesirable things, is called *avoidance-avoidance conflict*. If a person moves toward *B*, the force away from *B* increases, and he will tend to move back toward *A*. One possible result of this stalemate is "leaving the field," that is, trying to avoid making the choice, if that is possible. In Figure 3 it can be seen that if the person starts moving up or down, the directions of the forces are such as to accelerate that movement (represented by dotted lines). Question: Should I study for math or for Spanish? Answer: I'll go to a movie!

Approach-avoidance conflict has a single region with both positive and negative valence and forces toward and away from it. You meet a lot of nice people in a dormitory (+) but you don't have much freedom or privacy (−). Again, this conflict is not easily resolved, for moving toward *A* increases the force away from *A*. Since it also increases the force toward *A*, the result is continued conflict but with increasing intensity. *Double approach-avoidance* presents a choice between two regions, each of which has positive and negative value. This complicated type is perhaps more typical of human decision-making situations than the others. Finally, the approach-avoidance conflict need not involve a single region. Consider the case in which a university degree requirement is satisfied (+) only by a course you dislike (−). This state of affairs is represented in the last diagram in Figure 3. To get to *A* (+), the person must pass through *B* (−). He could move to *C*, which might be another course to which he is attracted or indifferent, but that course will not satisfy the degree requirement: a fact indicated by the impermeable boundary (barrier) between *C* and *A*.

There are obviously other kinds of conflict in addition to the ones mentioned, and, of course, not all behavior involves conflict in this sense. This discussion, however, introduces the common forms of conflict that lead to considerable research in the area of intrapersonal processes and illustrate the manner in which Lewin used his basic constructs to understand human behavior.

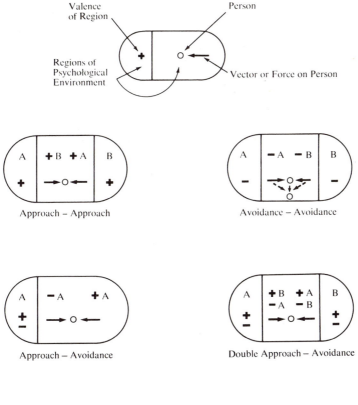

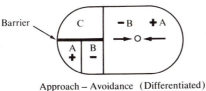

Approach – Avoidance (Differentiated)

Figure 3

Types of intrapersonal conflict.

UNCOMPLETED TASKS

While stemming from Lewin's approach, the study of the effect of interruption of some task is more commonly associated with Zeigarnik (1927). The finding that experimental subjects are more likely to recall uncompleted tasks has been labeled the *Zeigarnik effect*. Ovsiankina (1928) showed that subjects also were more likely to return to uncompleted tasks if given a choice among completed and uncompleted tasks. In terms of Lewin's theory, a need to finish the task is elicited by beginning it. Completion has the effect of reducing the inner-personal tension associated with that need. If the task is not completed, the tension remains; hence the vector-force remains, pushing the person toward the region representing that task. While this result may be intuitively plausible, one could well make a case for the opposite result: subjects will remember and want to return to "successes." Indeed, there can be no question that sometimes the Zeigarnik effect will appear while at other times the recall of completed tasks will be superior. For example, if the experimenter instructs the subjects to remember all tasks, a need (intention) is created that applies to both completed and uncompleted tasks. Reducing the pressure from such an instruction should increase the Zeigarnik effect. On the other hand, if not finishing a task is seen as "personal failure" or as a threat to self-esteem, subjects may recall more completed tasks (Deutsch, 1954).

LEVEL OF ASPIRATION

If a person is engaged in a task that has varying degrees of difficulty, an important theoretical and practical question to ask is: At what level of difficulty does he choose to perform? A student, for example, must decide whether he wants to attempt the pre-med program (high difficulty) or to enter the vocational training program (low difficulty). Will he stand five or fifty feet from the dartboard?

The choice the person makes from among several possibilities varying in difficulty is called his level of aspiration. In simple terms, the choice is made on the basis of relative valences between two levels. Each level has two valences, one (positive) for success and one (negative) for failure. The more difficult degrees in a task have a higher valence for success and lower valence for failure. To hit the bull's-eye at fifty feet, for example, is great (high valence for success), but if you miss, you don't feel too badly (low valence for failure).

If this were the only consideration, every student would be in pre-med, and nobody would stand closer than fifty feet to the dartboard. There is another consideration: to what extent is success at this level *probable*. In Lewinian terms, the subjective probability of success determines the *potency* of a situation. In everyday terms, success that is highly improbable will not be chosen over reasonably probable success even though the improbable success is much more highly valued.

People, then, tend to aspire to levels that are close to their performance level in the past. Because of some kind of a "self-improvement" norm, most aspire to a level slightly higher than their past performance but not so much higher as to be improbable. The valence of any level is a function of many things, culturally and personally determined. Group standards, for example, influence valence by producing high positive valence for performance better than average and high negative valence for performance worse than average. The nature of a person's self-image is a personal determinant.

When the concept of potency was introduced (Escalona, 1940) it had more general significance in the theory. It referred to "effective presence" of a region in the psychological environment. In situations where one might define success and failure, potency had to do with the question of whether the person saw the situation as a chance to be competent or as one in which he could make a fool of himself. For many such situations, subjective expectancy (probability) seems more or less equivalent to potency. With greater elaboration by Festinger (1942), the conceptual analysis of aspiration level took the following form:

$$\text{Force toward Level } A = \left(\begin{array}{c} \text{Potency of Success} \\ \text{at } A \end{array} \times \begin{array}{c} \text{Valence of} \\ \text{Success at } A \end{array} \right)$$

$$\left(\begin{array}{c} \text{Potency of Failure} \\ \text{at } A \end{array} \times \begin{array}{c} \text{Valence of} \\ \text{Failure at } A \end{array} \right) = \left(\begin{array}{c} \text{Expectancy of} \\ \text{Success at } A \end{array} \times \begin{array}{c} \text{Valence of} \\ \text{Success at } A \end{array} \right)$$

$$\left(\begin{array}{c} \text{Expectancy of} \\ \text{Failure at } A \end{array} \times \begin{array}{c} \text{Valence of} \\ \text{Failure at } A \end{array} \right)$$

According to this formulation, the level to which a person aspires will be that for which the force indicated in the equation is the greatest. The formula states that if a person expects to succeed, the valence for success will have more weight than the valence for failure; the "success" is more potent (effectively present) in his psychological environment.

Conceptualization of aspiration level in this manner turned out to be not only useful in explaining experimental results but also influential in later theories dealing with similar phenomena. Current notions about achievement motivation, for example, owe much to the earlier Lewinian work, as can be seen in Atkinson's work (see Chapter 12).

SUMMARY

In the sense of influencing other theories and also in the sense of important research based on the theory, Lewin's certainly ranks among the best in personology. We have discussed only intrapersonal conflict, interrupted activities, and level of aspiration, but research in other areas—such as social power and group dynamics; satiation-boredom; frustration-regression; substitution of one activity for another; social action and the study of behavioral settings—is also directly related to

Lewinian thought. Lewin is a part-father, at least, to current research on cognitive dissonance (see Chapter 13), the motive to achieve (see Chapter 12), and interpersonal conflict (Deutsch), just to mention a few. "The large sweep of Lewin's work, the brilliant innovations in many areas of psychology, cannot help but be impressive" (Deutsch, 1954, p. 219).

The theory itself does not seem to be enough to hold responsible for its great impact. Persons, need-tensions, valances and regions, and vectors: a simple theory. No doubt Lewin the man was partly responsible for the impact, exciting bright young scholars and facilitating their thought and research. But the theory clearly was facilitatory also, for reasons that are not hard to identify but are hard to understand. Lewin did not say much that had not been said before, but he said it in a new and different way. Why a slight change in the meaning of traditional constructs (such as placing the effect of needs in the valence construct) results in an explosion of research, and in personologists looking in completely new directions is a question best answered by philosophers. Whatever the answer, Lewin's contribution to personology must be judged significant.

REFERENCES

Deutsch, M. Field theory in social psychology. In G. Lindzey(Ed.), *Handbook of Social Psychology*, Vol. I. Cambridge, Mass.: Addison-Wesley, 1954.

Escalona, S. K. The effect of success and failure upon the level of aspiration and behavior in manic-depressive psychoses. *University of Iowa Studies of Child Welfare*, 1940, **16**, 199–307.

Festinger, L. A theoretical interpretation of shifts in level of aspiration. *Psychological Review*, 1942, **49**, 235–250.

Karsten, A. Psychische Sättigung. *Psychologische Forschung*, 1928, **10**, 142–254.

Lewin, K. *A dynamic theory of personality*. New York: McGraw-Hill, 1935.

Lewin, K. *Principles of topological psychology*. New York: McGraw-Hill, 1936.

Lewin, K. *The conceptual representation and the measurement of psychological forces*. Durham, N. C.: Duke Univ. Press, 1938.

Lewin, K. *Field theory in social science*. New York: Harper, 1951.

Ovsiankina, M. Die Wiederaufnahme von unterbrochenen Handlungen. *Psychologische Forschung*, 1928, **11**, 302–379.

Zeigarnik, B. Über das Behalten von erledigten und unerledigten Handlungen. *Psychologische Forschung*, 1927, **9**, 1–85.

The notion that a person tells you something about himself by the way he describes someone or something is certainly not new in psychology. Projective tests, such as the Thematic Apperception Test (TAT) and the Rorschach "ink blots," are based on the assumption that basic personality characteristics determine perception and description. Murphy's theory of autism (see Chapter 3) similarly depicts an influence of personal variables (needs) on perception of the environment. George Kelly, however, was the first to develop these notions into a systematic theory of personality.

Since its formulation in 1955, Kelly's theory has been growing in prominence, aided by certain research and a reformulation in thinking about "personality traits"—always one of the basic units in the minds of personologists. Traits, previously conceived of as general and stable dispositions, have in general been shown by research to be relatively specific and unstable (Mischel, 1968). In a word, a very important American word, traits weren't "working" as they should; they didn't predict behavior. A number of psychologists began considering the possibility that traits might better be seen as "conceptual categories" rather than as "attributes." For example, person A observes person B and then labels him "lazy" (a trait). Psychologists would then study B to see if he was indeed lazy. They would generally find no such evidence, or, at best, weak indications. Now, however, psychologists are beginning to study person A to see if his tendency to conceptualize people on a dimension of "lazy-energetic" has meaning for his life. Kelly's theory fully supports such a trend.

The theory, as our examples suggest, is primarily concerned with the way in which an individual perceives his world and with the effect of his perceptions on his behavior. According to Kelly, men organize their environment perceptually on the basis of *personal constructs,* that is, dimensions or categories of description. A teacher who sees all students as either lazy or energetic would be quite different from one who "construed" (perceptually constructed) students as either bland or creative. We are not here concerned with what the students actually are but rather with the teachers—how they see things, their conceptual categories.

The psychology of personal constructs is based, too, on a view of man as a scientist—that is, as someone who is in the business of predicting and controlling the events that occur in his environment. A person tries to estimate what will happen if he does this or that, and he makes his estimate on the basis of *his* theory of the world. Personal constructs, thus, are theoretical constructs as well as conceptual categories. I might conceive of two types of people, good people and bad people, and on that basis predict, say, that being honest "works" with the goods but not with the bads.

Kelly set down his theory in terms of one fundamental postulate and eleven corollaries, an outline we will follow in describing his theory in detail.

BASIC THEORY

Fundamental Postulate: *"A person's processes are psychologically channelized by the ways in which he anticipates events"* (1955, p. 46). Roughly translated, this means that behavior is determined by the ways in which the person predicts future occurrences. The "ways" are described in the first corollary.

Construction Corollary: *"A person anticipates events by construing their replications"* (1955, p. 50). "Construing replications" means that the individual's personal constructs are designed to note similarities and differences in events in order to predict when a "replication" will occur. No two events are exactly alike, of course, so replications must be defined by certain essential concepts. "An angry dog bites." The construing of anger (and of "dog-ness" and "biting") enables a prediction of attack even if this particular dog has never before been encountered.

Individuality Corollary: *"Persons differ from each other in their construction of events"* (1955, p. 55). There are individual differences.

Organization Corollary: *"Each person characteristically evolves for his convenience in anticipating events, a construction system embracing ordinal relationships between constructs"* (1955, p. 56). This corollary, in effect, asserts that the individual's constructs do not exist independently of one another. Instead they are organized, just as constructs in a theory are organized. The corollary thus identifies, for each individual, a personal theory about the world, complete with constructs and hypothesized relationships (organization). In the term "ordinal relationship," Kelly means to emphasize the hierarchical structure of an individual's theory, that is, its organization into very general to very specific constructs. For example, "good-bad" for many people is a very general construct that typically subsumes many other constructs, at least in part. "Good" may be highly related to "kind," "intelligent," and "religious"; "bad" to their psychological opposites. "Good," however, being more general, is a higher order construct (higher in ordinal status).

Dichotomy Corollary: *"A person's construction system is composed of a finite number of dichotomous constructs"* (1955, p. 59). The importance of this statement is contained in the word "dichotomous." The nature of human constructs, according to Kelly, is such that, explicitly or implicitly, three "things" are involved. A and B have some attribute in common and that attribute is psychologically opposite to what C is like. John and Sam are kind, while Bob is cruel. The two (A and B) are necessary because the construct is necessarily an abstraction depicting similarity between at least two things. The *contrast* (C) is necessary to define the opposite pole of the construct and hence define the construct as a whole.

The suggestion that people construe their world in dichotomies rather than on continuous dimensions is not so much an argument as it is a way of formulating his theory that Kelly found useful in treating patients; Kelly does claim, however, that most people see things in an either-or manner. In the clinic, for example, one might encounter a patient who claims that "All people are good." By Kelly's theory and by the definition of a construct, this is an incomplete construct because it has no contrast. The therapist may assume, therefore, that the contrast is implied or even unconscious. Something must be "bad" or the statement makes no sense. The patient may be suggesting that he is "bad"; or he may, in effect, be asking the therapist to list "bad" things for him. Which interpretation to follow is ascertained by further inquiry during the therapy session.

Choice Corollary: *"A person chooses for himself that alternative in a dichotomized construct through which he anticipates the greater possibility for extension and definition of his system"* (1955, p. 64). In a sense, this corollary is the most important since it describes the process through which behavior is produced. In Kelly's words:

If a person's processes are psychologically channelized by the ways in which he anticipates events, and those ways present themselves in dichotomous form, it follows that he must choose between the poles of his dichotomies in a manner which is predicted by his anticipations. We assume, therefore, that whenever a person is confronted with the opportunity for making a choice, he will tend to make that choice in favor of the alternative which seems to provide the best basis for anticipating the ensuing events.

Here is where inner turmoil so frequently manifests itself. Which shall a man choose, security or adventure? Shall he choose that which may eventually give him a wider understanding? For the man of constricted outlook whose world begins to crumble, death may appear to provide the only immediate certainty which he can lay hands on. And yet, in the words of Shakespeare's Hamlet,

But that the dread of something after death—
The undiscover'd country, from whose bourn
No traveler returns—puzzles the will;
And makes us rather bear those ills we have
Than fly to others that we know not of?

Whatever the breadth of his viewpoint, it is our assumption that man makes his choice in such a fashion as to enhance his anticipations. If he constricts his field of vision, he can turn his attention toward the clear definition of his system of constructs. If he is willing to tolerate some day-by-day uncertainties, he may broaden his field of vision and thus hope to extend the predictive range of the system. Whichever his choice may be—for constricted certainty or for broadened understanding—his decision is essentially elaborative. (1955, pp. 64–65)

Range Corollary: *"A construct is convenient for the anticipation of a finite range of events only"* (1955, p. 68). Any given construct, in other words, can be applied only to certain things. "Black-white" cannot be applied to the red tomato. "Male-female" is not used for rocks. Individuals may differ in range for the same construct, as with "respect-contempt": A very sensitive person may construe almost all behaviors toward him as one or the other, while a less sensitive person construes behaviors of much more limited range in these terms.

Experience Corollary: *"A person's construction system varies as he successively construes the replications of events"* (1955, p. 72). This is the learning corollary; it states that prior experience affects the present construct system. Those constructs found to be useful (not necessarily pleasurable) are retained; those that are not, are not retained. If this is learning, however, it is perceptual learning and, in many instances, is subject to more rapid change.

Modulation Corollary: *"The variation in a person's construction system is limited by the permeability of the constructs within whose range of convenience the variants lie"* (1955, p. 77). Permeable means here "open" to the introduction of new events or constructs. People in therapy, in Kelly's view, are often troubled by impermeable constructs, that is, they are unable to construe new events or reconstrue old events in a way that would promote more effective adjustment. The role of this corollary in the theory, however, is to assert that the organized system of constructs itself determines the learning that will occur. In function, the corollary is similar to Allport's propriate learning—the *organization* of previous learning has a profound effect upon subsequent learning.

Fragmentation Corollary: *"A person may successively employ a variety of construction subsystems which are inferentially incompatible with each other"* (1955, p. 83). Any theory which is based on organization must contain at least a note stating that the user of the theory must not be misled; organization may be an important, perhaps the most important, principle on which to base predictions, but organization is never complete. Integration of the various ways of construing the world is not perfect. The fragmentation corollary serves this function in Kelly's theory. In addition, with emphasis on the words *successively* and *subsystem*, this corollary warns us against seeing "consistency" only in replication of minor behaviors. For example, in Kelly's illustration, the fact that a person sucks his thumb 15 hours a day as a child does not mean he will suck his thumb 15 hours a day as an adult. How a person construes his environment and appropriate behaviors may be consistent, at least at higher "system levels," while the exhibited behaviors are not.

Commonality Corollary: *"To the extent that one person employs a construction of experience which is similar to that employed by another, his psychological processes are similar to those of the other person"* (1955, p. 90). Two people who view the world in the same way are likely to act similarly. The point to note in this corollary is that the important similarity is in the *construction* of the experience, not in the experience itself. If two people, for whatever reasons, are led to construe the world similarly, they will behave in a similar manner. Their prior *actual* experiences may have been completely different.

Sociality Corollary: *"To the extent that one person construes the construction processes of another, he may play a role in a social process involving the other person"* (1955, p. 95). The "social psychology corollary," as Kelly terms it, suggests that interpersonal interaction consists primarily of one person trying to understand how another is perceiving his environment. If you had such information, you would be able to more accurately predict the behavior of the other person. What he is likely to do and how it will affect you, is the core of interpersonal process, in Kelly's terms. So much is not surprising. But, again, note the emphasis on construction rather than on "reality." You may "misconstrue" —guess wrong about the other person—and still become involved in significant social interaction. Your "role" (the "appropriate" behaviors in terms of your perceptions) may be objectively realistic or objectively inappropriate. Since your behaviors are a prime determinant of the other's actions, you become involved in "a social process"—a sequence of interdependent behaviors.

THEORY EXPLICATION

Kelly's fundamental postulate and its eleven corollaries identify construction of experience as the prime determinant of behavior. They provide for individual differences and for social communication. They describe the nature, the structure, and the alteration of constructs. They are the basic theory. The remainder of Kelly's theory is largely concerned with explications of the basic theory as it has meaning for the clinical or therapeutic setting. Our treatment will discuss three of these explications: (1) the meaning of some standard theoretical terms in Kelly's theory, (2) fixed-role therapy, and (3) a commonly used criterion measure called the Role Construct Repertory Test.

THEORETICAL TERMS

"Anxiety is the recognition that the events with which one is confronted lie outside the range of convenience of one's construct system" (Kelly 1955, p. 495, italics deleted). *Anxiety* is a standard theoretical term found in almost every theory. The above quote translates it into Kelly's theory. The quote suggests that anxiety is similar to "uncertainty of prediction" and to a lack of perceptible means of dealing with, or at least understanding, a situation with which one is presented. An unfamiliar stimulus, for example, one for which no labels have been created, is likely to be frightening to most people.

Guilt is another standard theoretical term. In Kelly's view, guilt is the perception that your *core role* has not been followed. A role, in turn, is behavior that is based on the construction of other people's construction processes (sociality corollary). A core role is an important role, one that defines your identity. The child construes the parents' thinking and, on this basis, is identified as the parents' child. Rebellion, in the sense of acting as if your parents are not your parents will produce guilt: your core role will have been violated.

Hostility is a "continued effort to extort validational evidence" for a "social prediction which has already proved itself a failure" (1955, p. 510, italics deleted). Here we have a good example of how a new approach can cause one to view old ideas in a new way. Hostility, which is usually seen as an intent to do harm, becomes an attempt to hold on to invalid constructs. Change in constructs is difficult, effortful, sometimes impossible; how much better if we could change the world to fit our conceptions of it! Hostility, in Kelly's theory, is such an attempt. A father finds his college-age son living a life of a freethinker, with whatever physical characteristics (hair, clothes, and so forth) are appropriate to the time you are reading this sentence; his conception of his son, however, is roughly given by a picture of a bright-eyed boy scout. His response? He blows his top. He is not trying to injure his son, he is trying to "extort validation evidence."

FIXED-ROLE THERAPY

A patient in therapy is someone who has found his constructs at least ineffective enough to cause him to seek help. If the therapist is operating with the psychology of personal constructs, he sees his goal, in gross terms, as aiding the patient in altering his construct system so that it is more adaptable. How does the therapist accomplish this feat? One answer given by Kelly is fixed-role therapy, presented in this text because of its obvious relationship to Kelly's basic theory.

In essence, the therapist presents to the patient a role (in the theatrical sense) and asks him to play that role for a time. The role is designed to pressure the client into constructions of his experience that will be beneficial for his personal adjustment. It gives him a chance to "try things out," protected by the authority of the therapist and the recognition that the role is "just make-believe." But the construed experiences he will have will presumably alleviate the problems that forced him into therapy in the first place. Have you ever acted? Have you ever read a play or novel and identified so strongly with the hero that you found it influencing the way you perceived things the next day? This is the experience that Kelly wanted to create for his patient, an experience designed for the patient's particular needs.

Writing the role-sketch entails some diagnostic evidence about the way the patient presently construes his experiences, and some judgments about how such constructions are likely to lead to anxiety, depression, or the like. The role-sketch then asks him to act in such a way that the "pathogenic" constructions are altered, or tested in such a way as to point out their deficiencies. Very often, the patient is asked to make believe he is just the opposite of what he perceives himself to be. If he is submissive, he is told to act dominant. This "opposite" portrayal aligns itself in Kelly's theory with the notion that people use dichotomous constructs in their thinking and that for this reason sharp contrast is more valuable than slight modification. The sketch is formulated in such a way that the patient can relatively easily see the consequences of the role; in scientific terms, the constructs are chosen so that they are empirically testable, even though here we are talking of tests made by a single person.

ROLE CONSTRUCT REPERTORY TEST

This test was developed by Kelly and his associates to assess the personal constructs used by an individual in his perception of experience. More particularly, the Rep Test, as it is commonly called, is designed to elicit the "characterizing constructs" one uses in the description of *roles*. The subject is given a list of roles, such as "a teacher you liked," "your brother nearest your age (or the person who has been most like a brother)," "a neighbor whom you find hard to understand," and so forth. He is asked to write the name of a person he knows who fits the role description. Then groups of three out of the approximately 25 role-people are presented to the subject (see Kelly, 1955, pp. 222 ff).

The subject is asked to state in what important way two of the three are alike but different from the third. This is a construct. To complete the construct, he is asked for the contrast—that is, the examiner asks in what way the third role-person is different. My mother and sister are alike in that they are "kind," and they are unlike someone else who is "cruel."

Again, it must be emphasized that Kelly is not concerned with the attributes of your mother; the goal is to assess the constructs you use to perceive your world. "Kind-cruel" is the goal.

The Rep Test has not been standardized to the extent that many tests have been. Experimenters usually vary the number and content of the roles to suit their purposes. Other forms of the test have been used, such as the "grid form," in which each role-person is considered for each construct as to whether the construct or contrast applies, even though the construct came from different comparisons. An excellent review of research on the Rep Test along with studies on the basic theory is available in Bonarius (1965).

One notable product of Kelly's theory in general and the Rep Test in particular is the "trait" of *cognitive complexity*. The most common indicator variable is roughly the number of different constructs produced in the Rep Test. In other words, if a person uses a great number of constructs in describing people, it is inferred that he is more cognitively complex than someone who is limited in descriptive categories. If I saw everyone I knew as either good or bad and used no other designation, I would be low in cognitive complexity. Bieri (1961) has reviewed relevant research, which is generally concerned with the relation of this variable to social perception and social prediction. Bieri (1955), for example, found that subjects high in cognitive complexity were more accurate in predicting how classmates would answer a questionnaire. Those low in cognitive complexity tended to simply guess that the classmate would answer as they would answer.

SUMMARY

The organized theory that is Kelly's is a good example of theories built around a single idea. In this case, the question is, "What would happen if we thought of traits as conceptual categories rather than as attributes?" The answer is described in this chapter. In broad summary, the scientist looks at different people—at the rater rather than at the person being rated, for example. He looks at the person in different ways: not as an animal or as a god, but as a scientist like himself, who is trying to predict and control his personal environment. The "personal" personality theory and its constructs become objects of study.

Such a view of man does not concern itself much with traditional questions of motivation and learning, at least not in traditional ways. Traditional phenomena, such as anxiety, guilt, and hostility, are re-interpreted; new methods of assessment and therapy follow from the theory. In the end, however, the elaboration of the fundamental postulate can hardly be more than a beginning. How personal constructs are developed and how they relate to behavior, for example, are questions for which Kelly's insight is at best weak. This is to be expected, of course, since these questions demand experimental treatment. Kelly has given us the power of a new idea; that is quite enough for one lifetime.

REFERENCES

Bieri, J. Cognitive complexity-simplicity and predictive behavior. *Journal of Abnormal and Social Psychology*, 1955, **51**, 263–268.

Bieri, J. Complexity-simplicity as a personality variable in cognitive and preferential behavior. In D. W. Fiske & S. Maddi (Eds.), *Functions of varied experience*. Homewood, Ill.: Dorsey, 1961.

Bonarius, J. C. J. Research in the personal construct theory of George A. Kelly. In B. A. Maher (Ed.), *Progress in experimental personality research*. Vol. II. New York: Academic Press, 1965.

Kelly, G. A. *The psychology of personal constructs*. Vol. I. New York: Norton, 1955.

Mischel, W. *Personality and assessment*. New York: Wiley, 1968.

Like Festinger's theory of cognitive dissonance (see Chapter 13), Atkinson's theory of achievement motivation is not usually considered a theory of personality. Both have had a marked influence on personality research, however. Atkinson, in addition, in the course of understanding achievement motivation, has developed notions of motivation in general that could well serve as a complete personality theory if the necessary applications were made.

Of the so-called human needs, certainly one of the more important is the need for achievement. To the extent to which people differ in this need, they presumably differ in performance, persistence, and actual achievement—in short, in the productive activities that mark progress both for the individual and society. To understand the workings of this need, David McClelland, John Atkinson, and co-workers Clark and Lowell began a systematic program of study, with the first major publication in 1953. The first problem was to develop a suitable criterion measure for the achievement need. The Thematic Apperception Test (TAT) developed by Murray (see Chapter 4), who also discussed the need for achievement, was the instrument of choice. In the TAT, people view a series of lifelike drawings and then are asked to construct a story about the pictures. Who are the people? What is happening? What led up to the present event, and what will follow? It is assumed that in constructing their stories the storytellers will use themes that represent concerns in their own lives; they will "display" their own unique personalities (including needs) in their stories.

In order to develop a more rigorous measure, Atkinson and McClelland (1948) asked subjects to tell stories after 1, 4, and 16 hours of food deprivation. The goal, of course, was not to develop a measure of need for food, but to analyze the difference in the stories when a relatively clearly defined need had been induced. This information would give the researchers leads as to what to look for with other needs such as the need for achievement. They found that the most notable increase with hours of deprivation was in the subject's concern with food deprivation and in instrumental activities designed to obtain food. They did not find increases in food imagery and other goal-attainment themes.

This procedure was then extended to the field of need for achievement. Basically, the experimental design was the same: stories from people who had undergone treatment to induce weak achievement needs were compared with stories in which strong needs were presumed. In both cases, a series of "intelligence" tests were administered before the TAT task. To induce weak need, these tests were described as in a developmental stage; subjects were asked *not* to sign their names; and the experimenter was informally dressed—all aspects of a "relaxed" situation. To induce achievement orientation, the formally-dressed experimenter described the test as one of great importance; subjects were to sign their names on all forms. The differences between stories were carefully analyzed. In similar fashion, comparisons were made between stories written by subjects given the impression of failure or success (false norms) just before taking the TAT. From comparisons of this type, a scoring key for TAT stories was developed (see Atkinson, 1958a).

The next steps were to investigate the reliability and validity of the newly created measure. The coding (scoring) of the stories was found to be concrete enough (after training) to produce more than acceptable levels of inter-coder agreement. The reliability picture was less encouraging. Lowell (1950), for example, found that the degree to which two assessments of need for achievement agreed was .22, a correlation coefficient both low and statistically insignificant. More sophisticated analyses by Haber and Alpert (1958) suggest reliability ranges from around .50 to .75, depending on the nature of the pictures used in the TAT. Nevertheless, the reliability of the TAT achievement measure remains a controversial issue, one to which we will return in a later section. Suffice it to say here that even in the Lowell study it was discovered that almost 75% of the subjects who scored in the top or bottom half in the first administration were in the same half in the second testing. Many studies therefore classified subjects either as "high" or "low" in the need to achieve; individual scores within these categories were disregarded.

The next question to be asked concerned the validity of the TAT scoring procedure—that is, whether the test measured what the researchers thought it measured. A TAT score is supposed to be an indication of the need to achieve, which should be related to actual achievement behavior. Hence, Lowell (1952) found that persons scoring high on the TAT performed better on arithmetic and verbal tasks. Rosen (1958) found that students who did not aspire to go beyond high school tended to score low on the TAT. These and a number of similar studies (reviewed in McClelland et al., 1953) involved empirical relationships of interest, but the theoretical relationships are approximately what one would expect if the TAT were really a measure of the need to achieve.

The development of the theory as we know it today was based

on the initial reliability and validity studies, of course; but the study of *risk-taking* was the area in which the most important advances were made. McClelland, who is in a sense the father of the achievement motive, had strong interests in the social antecedents (child training) and social consequences (industrial output) of entrepreneurial activities and has since moved to the level of sociological study (McClelland, 1961). Atkinson had similar interests in risk-taking, but he focused on the psychological theory of motivation, which is basically the attempt to explain the correlations between TAT scores and behavior. This psychological theory is the subject of the next section.

Before we get to the theory, however, we should indicate what the theory sought to explain. One might expect that the higher a person's need for achievement, the greater the risk he will take. That such is not the case might have been predicted by previous "level of aspiration" studies (see Lewin, Chapter 10) in which it was found that most people tend to take moderate rather than extreme chances. McClelland (1958), in a study of children, expected and found that those high in need achievement played from "middle" positions in a game of ringtoss, while "low" subjects played at the extreme (very close or very far) positions. Atkinson (1958b) was at the same time finding that subjects worked hardest when the probability of their work earning a reward was .50. Clark, Teevan, and Ricciuti (1958) were concurrently discovering that students with "realistic" grade aspirations were highest in the TAT scores for need achievement. From these and other studies, the summary statement was clear: Those people high in need for achievement prefer moderate risks, while "lows" will choose either very low or very high risk. In short, this is the "fact" that led to the current theory of achievement motivation.

ATKINSON'S THEORY OF ACHIEVEMENT MOTIVATION

The most complete statement of the theory of achievement motivation is stated in Atkinson (1964). A somewhat briefer statement is found in Atkinson and Feather (1966, chapters 1 and 20). The "facts to be explained," apart from the tendency to choose moderate risks, are the "direction, magnitude, and persistence of behavior" in situations "when an individual knows that his performance will be evaluated (by himself or by others) in terms of some standard of excellence and that the consequence of his actions will be either a favorable evaluation (success) or an unfavorable evaluation (failure)" (Atkinson, 1964, pp. 240–241).

The variables of the situation that are important for achievement motivation are identified as *incentive* and *expectancy* (subjective probability). What are the chances of success in the task? And what is the success worth (incentive) if it is achieved? Together with the *motive* to achieve success, these three variables combine to determine the tendency to "approach success" or, in other words, to perform. The following formula summarizes this relationship:

$$T_s = M_s \times P_s \times I_s$$

where T = tendency to approach success
             M = motive
             P = subjective probability
             I = incentive

A "tendency" corresponds to what common sense would call "an urge to do something." It will result in behavior unless some other tendency is stronger.

This relationship was simplified by the work of Festinger, Escalona, and Lewin on "level of aspiration," who found that task incentive was related to task difficulty. From this, Atkinson assumed that incentive I could be expressed in terms of subjective probability P. The harder the task, the less the probability of success and the more the incentive for success; hence incentive was expressed as $1 - P_s$.

Let us observe this theoretical formulation as it is applied to a risk-taking situation. Assume that people are playing a ringtoss game in which they may choose the distance from which they will toss the ring. Position A is very close; the probability of success P_s therefore is high, but the incentive $1 - P_s$ is low. Position E is very distant; the expectancy is low, the incentive value is high. Table 1 gives the probabilities of success as they might be perceived by subjects and enters them into the formula. Illustrations are given for two subjects: one with a low motive to achieve ($M_s = 1$) and one who is a more highly motivated subject ($M_s = 8$).

Table 1

Analysis of tendency to achieve success at various distances from the peg in a ringtoss game. (Adapted from Atkinson, 1964, p. 242, with permission of D. Van Nostrand Co.)

POSITION	P_s	$I_s = 1 - P_s$	$T_s = M_s \times P_s \times I_s$ T_s when $M_s = 1$	T_s when $M_s = 8$
A (close)	.90	.10	.09	.72
B	.70	.30	.21	1.68
C	.50	.50	.25	2.00
D	.30	.70	.21	1.68
E (distant)	.10	.90	.09	.72

Table 1 shows that both individuals depicted would choose to play at position C, where the tendency to approach success is greatest (.25 and 2.00). In other words, the achievement motive predisposes people to play at positions where the chances of success are neither too low ("just luck") nor too high ("anybody could have done it"). They prefer to play at an intermediate level where personal ability has meaning and where success reflects on them. Comparing the tendencies when $M_s = 1$ with those when $M_s = 8$, we note that the preference for intermediate levels is more pronounced when $M_s = 8$. Subjects with weaker motives in an experimental setting are somewhat more indifferent in their preferences toward various positions. Also, T_s for $M_s = 8$ exceeds T_s for $M_s = 1$ at all positions, but the difference is largest at the intermediate levels. We would therefore predict that subjects with stronger motives will perform markedly better only at intermediate positions in a ringtoss game where every player is forced to play at all positions.

Achievement-oriented behavior concerns itself not only with the general tendency to achieve success but also with the tendency to *avoid failure*. Whereas the motive to achieve may be characterized as a capacity for reacting with pride in accomplishment, the motive to avoid failure may be characterized as a capacity for reacting with shame and embarrassment when the outcome of performance is failure. When this disposition is aroused within a person, the result is anxiety and a tendency to withdraw from the situation (Atkinson, 1964, p. 244).

The formula for the tendency to avoid failure is similar to the one for approaching success:

$$T_{-f} = M_{AF} \times P_f \times I_f$$

The probability of failure P_f is, of course, equal to $1 - P_s$. The incentive of failure I_f is negative incentive: Failure at an easy task is more shameful than failure at a difficult task, hence the incentive of failure is expressed as $I_f = -P_s$. A high probability of success results in a high incentive of failure, as can be seen in Table 2, which is patterned after Table 1 and uses the same values of P_s.

Table 2

Analysis of tendency to avoid failure at various distances from the peg in a ringtoss game. (Adapted from Atkinson, 1964, p. 244, with permission of D. Van Nostrand Co.)

POSITION	$P_f = 1 - P_s$	$I_f = -P_s$	$T_{-f} = M_{AF} \times P_f \times I_f$	
			T_{-f} WHEN $M_{AF} = 1$	T_{-f} WHEN $M_{AF} = 8$
A (close)	.10	−.90	−.09	−.72
B	.30	−.70	−.21	−1.68
C	.50	−.50	−.25	−2.00
D	.70	−.30	−.21	−1.68
E (distant)	.90	−.10	−.09	−.72

According to Table 2, the individuals represented would tend to avoid playing altogether (all tendencies are negative). If forced to choose, they would choose either the closest or the most distant position, where the tendencies are least negative. Again, the preference for extreme positions and the avoidance of intermediate positions will be most marked when the motive strength is high.

To summarize the implications of the theory in a ringtoss setting, we would expect that a person for whom the motive to achieve exceeds the motive to avoid failure will choose to play in the intermediate positions, while a person with a stronger motive to avoid failure will choose "unusual" positions: right next to the peg or as far away as he can get. What we have, of course, is a theory expressly designed to explain the results mentioned above. While the fact that the theory can "postdict" those results is therefore no surprise, a theory so generated can be used to predict new phenomena.

For example, Atkinson (1957) further explored the implications of actual success and failure in the ringtoss game. If the $M_s > M_{AF}$ person chooses position C and succeeds, where does he play next? Allowing the further assumption that actual success increases the perceived probability of success from any position, P_s at C might increase from .50 to .60, causing I_s to decrease to .40. (You will recall that $I_s = 1 - P_s$.) The result is that position C is now less desirable! Whereas formerly $T_s = .25$, in the new situation $T_s = 1 \times .60 \times .40 = .24$. The player will either stay at position C or switch to position D, where P_s also changes to .40; then I_s changes to .60 and $T_s = 24$. The opposite result is obtained if failure occurs at position C: there is an increased tendency to switch to B.

How about the subject for whom the motive to avoid failure is greater? He is playing, say, at the most difficult position, E, so $T_{-f} = 1 \times .90 \times -.10 = -.09$. He fails to ring the peg. Failure decreases P_s and increases P_f. T_{-f} now may equal $1 \times .95 \times -.05 = -.0475$. The position is now *less* undesirable. Success makes the choice less desirable for the $M_s > M_{AF}$ subjects, and failure makes the choice more desirable for $M_{AF} > M_s$ subjects. Nonobvious predictions like these are always exciting to the scientist and make the theory influential in vast areas of research.

Consider another possibility. The $M_{AF} > M_s$ subject plays at E and succeeds. P_f decreases. $T_{-f} = 1 \times .80 \times -.20 = -.16$. Success has made E more threatening. What does the subject do? The tendency for position A changes too, from $T_{-f} = -.09$ to $T_{-f} = 1 \times .05 \times -.95 = -.0475$. Position A increases in desirability when success occurs at position E. The subject is predicted to switch from E to A. He has just achieved a spectacular success at the most distant position; he then walks to the closest, easiest position for his next try. Partial confirmation of such predictions was obtained by Moulton (1966).

We have been discussing the theory of achievement motivation primarily in the context of the ringtoss game. Ringtoss games, of course, are not all that important; what is important is the characteristic of such games that expectancy and incentive are related. More precisely, such games are situations in which it is reasonable to assume that $I_s = 1 - P_s$. Many similar situations exist and are of considerable intrinsic importance to the individual and society; such situations can be called "ringtoss analogies."

One such analogy is the "game" of vocational or occupational choice. There is a dimension of "status" in such choices that runs roughly from "Supreme Court Justice" to "unskilled laborer." In choosing to try for any given vocation, there is an expectancy of success and an incentive, related to expectancy roughly as $1 - P_s$: the less chance of success, the more the incentive. Mahone (1960) studied the discrepancy between subjective estimates of one's own ability and estimates of the ability necessary to succeed vocations chosen as goals by a group of college students. The prediction was that people for whom $M_{AF} > M_s$ should show a very large or a very small discrepancy; in "ringtoss terms," they will choose an occupation that, given their ability level, is too easy or too difficult. The motive to achieve was measured by the TAT, the motive to avoid failure was indicated by scores on a "test-anxiety" measure. Dividing the distribution of discrepancy scores into thirds, 50% of the subjects high on TAT scores and low on test-anxiety fell into the middle third; only 18% of the low TAT, high test-anxiety subjects fell into that third.

As another example of a ringtoss analogy, O'Connor, Atkinson and Horner (1966) examined the effect of ability groupings in the educational system. Achievement theory predicts that people high in achievement motive perform best when the chances of success (getting good grades) are close to 50%. They assumed, then, that such people would perform better and show greater interest in a class composed of students of similar ability (homogeneous) than in a heterogeneous class. Results supported this hypothesis. The comparable hypothesis for students with high motivation to avoid failure was that they would perform at a lower level and show less interest in homogeneous classes, since the tendency to avoid failure is greatest at $P_s = .50$. The failure-oriented students did not show a decrement in performance, but there was evidence of a decline in interest.

Of the "facts to be explained" we have been introduced to both magnitude of behavior and direction (choice). The third fact, persistence, is comparably handled. An example, from the important work on this problem by Feather (1961), was an experimental setting in which subjects were given a series of puzzles. The first puzzle was actually impossible to solve, but subjects were told that either 5% usually solve it (difficult) or that 70% do so (easy). They could then make as many attempts at the first puzzle as they wanted, before moving on to the second. How many attempts they made was the criterion of persistence.

Predictions from the theory follow from the previously discussed effects of failure for $M_s > M_{AF}$ and $M_{AF} > M_s$ subjects. For $M_s > M_{AF}$, failure at an easy task ($P_s = .70$) should increase the desirability (if $P_s = .60$, then $T_s = .60 \times .40 \times M_s = .24M_s$, compared to $T_s = .70 \times .30 \times M_s = .21M_s$). The subject should persist. Failure at a difficult task makes the task less desirable. Conversely, $M_{AF} > M_s$ subjects should persist at .05 tasks following failure and should "move on" following failure at .70 tasks. The results confirmed the hypothesis: $M_{AF} > M_s$ subjects showed greater than average persistence at the difficult task while $M_s > M_{AF}$ subjects persisted at the easy task.

PROBLEMS AND PROSPECTS

Achievement theory, from its beginnings, has never involved self-conscious endeavor; rather, there has been a continuing effort to discuss problems openly and explicitly (a good example is found in chapter 20 of Atkinson and Feather, 1966). Problems and tentative solutions are given in such matters as the conceptualization, assessment, and induction of motive, incentive, expectancy, and other constructs. In all such discussions, the approach assumes that predicting, testing, and review is a never-ending effort with theory amplifying experimental data, and data reflecting back on theory. Often, for example, data change the theory in such a way as to suggest a solution to a problem that had been previously difficult to handle. As an illustration of such a process, we can return to the issue of whether the TAT operates as an adequate operational criterion for the motive to achieve success.

In theory, the TAT score measures the strength of M_s minus M_{AF}. Since the motive to avoid failure is an inhibitory (don't-do-it) tendency, it should result in avoidance of achievement themes in the TAT. If a person scores low in the TAT, therefore, it may reflect a high M_{AF}. If M_s is low, however, a low TAT score may simply reflect little orientation one way or the other toward achievement activities. The problem of independent assessment of M_s and M_{AF} remains an important one. Some studies have used the Test Anxiety Questionnaire (Mandler and Cowen, 1958) or the Debilitating Anxiety Scale (Alpert and Haber, 1960) as a separate indicator of M_{AF} in conjunction with TAT scores. A high TAT score plus low anxiety then becomes the clearest representative of $M_s > M_{AF}$, a low TAT and high anxiety the clearest representative of $M_{AF} > M_s$.

Alternatives to the TAT have also been tried, but without much success. Self-reports, objective tests, and peer ratings have not provided any consistent evidence of construct validity of the type provided by the TAT. The reliability controversy surrounding the TAT measure, however, makes the search for additional measures of continuing importance.

Reliability (the degree to which two testings of the same person agree) in any assessment device should be quite high; researchers like to have it around .90. Our better intelligence tests achieve such levels, and although it is not uncommon for useful personality tests to have lower reliabilities, the goal of very high reliability is always desirable. The TAT achievement measure has often been accused of uncommonly low reliability (Moss and Kagan, 1961; Kagan and Moss, 1959; Birney, 1959; Krumboltz and Farquhar, 1957), and even its advocates are sometimes plagued by low correlations (Lowell, 1950; Reitman and Atkinson, 1958). On the other hand, sometimes acceptable levels are reached, as by Atkinson (see Table 7.2 in McClelland et al., 1953) and by Haber and Alpert (1958). These latter studies tend to be generally superior in design and execution; hence advocates of the TAT tend to dismiss lower reliability as attributable to procedural deviations, inadequate training in the scoring method, and the like. With unusual care in the selection of TAT pictures and in the procedures of administration, it appears that one can attain reliabilities of around .75.

Whatever unreliability remains (apart from the question of whether it is a little or a lot) is also subject to various interpretations. Advocates (see Reitman and Atkinson, 1958) discuss a number of factors possibly responsible for decreased reliability, factors which, if truly present and taken into account, would increase reliability or diminish the scientific importance of low correlations. For example, they suggest that the TAT achievement score may be valid for the first four to six pictures and invalid thereafter. If this were true, one would obtain low reliability because a second administration would not be measuring the motive to achieve. Developmental studies involving repeated testing, of course, would then be suspect, but the single administration experiment would be admissible. Critics of the TAT, however, remain unconvinced (see Mischel, 1968). Indeed, it is well that they remain critical; it is up to the TAT advocates to put their speculation to experimental test.

In any case, alternative measures of the motive to achieve would be desirable. One possibility, developed in the course of research, has exciting potential. The study most directly concerned is one by Litwin

(1966), in which certain implicit notions of "value" contained in achievement theory were explored. The value of any event or object could be considered as the incentive, but this conception does not take into account the effect of motive strength. If one attempts to define incentive independently of motive, as achievement theory does, the value must be assumed to be some combination of motive strength and incentive. The general formula, $T_s = M_s \times E_s \times I_s$ can be written as $T_s = E_s \times (M_s \times I_s)$ or $T_s = E_s \times V_s$, where V_s (Value of success) $= M_s \times I_s$. In words, a steak is a steak (as incentive), but the value of a steak is greater to a hungry man than to one who is satiated (different motive strengths). Suppose we ask subjects to indicate their estimates of the "value" of success in a ringtoss game by having them assign a monetary prize from 0 to $1.00 for a ringer at each of the various positions. We would expect persons higher in M_s to assign higher prizes (values). This is roughly what Litwin found, as represented in Figure 4.

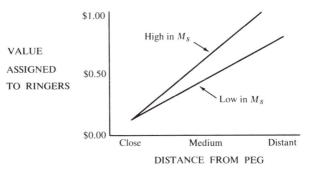

Figure 4

Estimates of "suitable" prizes for successful ring-tosses at various distances from the peg. (Adapted from Litwin, 1966, p. 112, with permission of John Wiley & Sons, Inc.)

These results are predicted by the theory, as can be shown by the example of $M_s = 1$ (low) and $M_s = 8$ (high). Value (that is $M_s \times I_s$) when incentive is low (close position) does not differ appreciably between the two motive strengths: $1 \times .10 = .10$, as compared to $8 \times .10 = .80$. When incentive is high, however, the difference is much greater: $1 \times .90 = .90$, $8 \times .90 = 7.20$.

The implications for the assessment of achievement motive are seen if we note that when we plot estimates of value along a dimension of incentive (distances in Figure 4), the *slope* of the line will tell us motive strength. Steep slopes indicate high M_s.

Working with very crude data, Morgan (1966) used this technique in a national survey of economic behavior. Using as the incentive a dimension of occupational status or prestige, informants were asked how they thought most people would feel if their son chose one of the various occupations. Figure 5 shows the expected results.

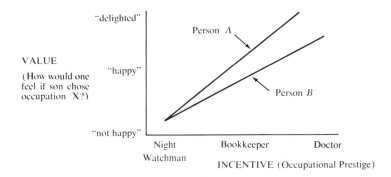

Figure 5

Hypothetical estimates of the value of various occupational levels. Illustrative values and occupations taken from Morgan (1966).

Person A would be assumed to be higher in M_s than person B. A measure indicating the slope of this assessment line for each individual was computed and found to be related to such indices of economic achievement as income and reported lack of limitation when faced with physical disability.

The "slope" index of the motive to achieve has not been widely used, but it is deserving of further research attention. What is interesting to note, however, is the source of the suggested measure in the theory itself. This interaction of theory and data, so characteristic of achievement theory in general, is social science at its best. And such interactions give promise that even theories with vague constructs and poor operational criteria can eventually "bootstrap" themselves into systems with finely tuned predictive power.

SUMMARY

The study of achievement behavior and the development of the theory of achievement motivation were and are an endeavor of many people. Atkinson and McClelland are handy labels to put on the theory; but here more than in most theories, labeling does a great injustice to the many talented scholars working in the same area. Even in a treatment without the convenient personal identifications, we would have had to slight the important and directly related work on similar motives: affiliation, power, and sex, for example. (See Birch and Veroff,

1966, in this series.) All of these people working in all of these areas have a common goal: the development of a general theory of motivation. If and when that goal is attained, achievement theory will become a full-fledged theory of personality.

Certainly, the theory as developed to encompass the motives to achieve and to avoid failure has implications for behaviors other than achievement. The general formula, which depicts instigation to action as a function of a motive, an expectancy, and an incentive, could be applied to almost any human behavior. Probably certain additional constructs will have to be added eventually, such as one to deal with the *availability* of a response (Birch and Veroff, 1966). As is, the theory deals only with choices among behaviors already in the repertoire of the person. Atkinson (1964) and Atkinson and Feather (1966) contain good discussions of the directions that such expansion of the theory may take.

The study of achievement motivation contains one of the best examples of approaches that postulate relatively general theoretical constructs such as "motive" or "trait." The motive is carefully defined, and the definition is constantly under scrutiny to see if it shouldn't be revised. Great care is taken to develop reasonable operational criteria, so much so that the criteria (TAT, for example) become objects of criticism while less rigorous theorists "get away" with using absurd measures totally free of any evidence of reliability and validity. The amount of research generated is phenomenal, and no contradictory evidence is dismissed without survey. The theory is constantly under revision, always subject to empirical evidence. The major studies are brought together every so often, so that other scientists can bring themselves up to date without looking through thirty different journals. These are serious and optimistic scholars, and the result reflects that fact.

REFERENCES

Alpert, R., & Haber, R. N. Anxiety in academic achievement situations. *Journal of Abnormal and Social Psychology*, 1960, **61**, 207–215.

Atkinson, J. W. Motivation determinants of risk-taking behavior. *Psychological Review*, 1957, **64**, 359–372.

Atkinson, J. W. (Ed.) *Motives in fantasy, action, and society*. Princeton, N. J.: Van Nostrand, 1958. (a)

Atkinson, J. W. Towards experimental analysis of human motivation in terms of motives, expectancies, and incentives. In J. W. Atkinson (Ed.), *Motives in fantasy, action, and society*. Princeton, N. J.: Van Nostrand, 1958. (b)

Atkinson, J. W. *An introduction to motivation.* Princeton, N. J.: Van Nostrand, 1964.

Atkinson, J. W., & Feather, N. T. (Eds.) *A theory of achievement motivation.* New York: Wiley, 1966.

Atkinson, J. W., & McClelland, D. C. The projective expression of needs. II. The effect of different intensities of the hunger drive on thematic apperception. *Journal of Experimental Psychology,* 1948, **38**, 643–658.

Birch, D., & Veroff, J. *Motivation: a study of action.* Belmont, Calif.: Brooks/Cole, 1966.

Birney, R. C. The reliability of the achievement motive. *Journal of Abnormal and Social Psychology,* 1959, **58**, 266–267.

Clark, R. A., Teevan, R., & Ricciuti, H. N. Hope of success and fear of failure as aspects of need for achievement. In J. W. Atkinson (Ed.), *Motives in fantasy, action, and society.* Princeton, N. J.: Van Nostrand, 1958.

Feather, N. T. The relationship of persistence at a task to expectation of success and achievement-related motives. *Journal of Abnormal and Social Psychology,* 1961, **63**, 552–561.

Haber, R. N., & Alpert, R. The role of situation and picture cues in projective measurement of the achievement motive. In J. W. Atkinson (Ed.), *Motives in fantasy, action, and society.* Princeton, N. J.: Van Nostrand, 1958.

Kagan, J., & Moss, H. A. Stability and validity of achievement fantasy. *Journal of Abnormal and Social Psychology,* 1959, **58**, 357–364.

Krumboltz, J. D., & Farquhar, W. W. Reliability and validity of the n-Achievement test. *Journal of Consulting Psychology,* 1957, **21**, 226–228.

Litwin, G. H. Achievement motivation, expectancy of success, and risk-taking behavior. In J. W. Atkinson & N. T. Feather (Eds.), *A theory of achievement motivation.* New York: Wiley, 1966.

Lowell, E. L. *A methodological study of projectively measured achievement motivation.* Unpublished master's thesis, Wesleyan University, 1950.

Lowell, E. L. The effect of need for achievement on learning and speed of performance. *Journal of Psychology,* 1952, **33**, 31–40.

McClelland, D. C. Risk taking in children with high and low need for achievement. In J. W. Atkinson (Ed.), *Motives in fantasy, action, and society.* Princeton, N. J.: Van Nostrand, 1958.

McClelland, D. C. *The achieving society.* Princeton, N. J.: Van Nostrand, 1961.

McClelland, D. C., Atkinson, J. W., Clark, R. A., & Lowell, E. L. *The achievement motive.* New York: Appleton-Century-Crofts, 1953.

Mahone, C. H. Fear of failure and unrealistic vocational aspiration. *Journal of Abnormal and Social Psychology,* 1960, **60**, 253–261.

Mandler, G., & Cowen, J. E. Test anxiety questionnaires. *Journal of Consulting Psychology,* 1958, **22**, 228–229.

Morgan, J. N. The achievement motive and economic behavior. In J. W. Atkinson & N. T. Feather (Eds.), *A theory of achievement motivation.* New York: Wiley, 1966.

Moss, H. A., & Kagan, J. Stability of achievement and recognition seeking behaviors from early childhood through adulthood. *Journal of Abnormal and Social Psychology,* 1961, **62,** 504–518.

Moulton, R. W. Effects of success and failure on level of aspiration as related to achievement motives. In J. W. Atkinson & N. T. Feather (Eds.), *A theory of achievement motivation.* New York: Wiley, 1966.

O'Connor, P., Atkinson, J. W., & Horner, M. Motivational implications of ability groupings in schools. In J. W. Atkinson & N. T. Feather (Eds.), *A theory of achievement motivation.* New York: Wiley, 1966.

Reitman, W. R., & Atkinson, J. W. Some methodological problems in the use of thematic apperceptive measures of human motives. In J. W. Atkinson (Ed.), *Motives in fantasy, action, and society.* Princeton, N. J.: Van Nostrand, 1958.

Rosen, B. C. The achievement syndrome: a psychocultural dimension of social stratification. In J. W. Atkinson (Ed.), *Motives in fantasy, action, and society.* Princeton, N. J.: Van Nostrand, 1958.

LEON FESTINGER

13

Notions of consistency have long been central in theories of personality. The "self," a common enough theoretical construct, functions largely to portray an organized and consistent set of subconstructs which dictates seeking, learning, and remembering of additional elements. Those elements which are consistent with the organized set are incorporated, while those which "clash" are rejected, distorted, and so forth. Allport's propriate learning is an example of such thinking.

Leon Festinger in 1957 put forward a highly influential theory of attitude change which also was about consistency. Though it is not usually considered a theory of personality, its widespread influence and the creative conceptualization of such a core construct have combined to make it a statement of importance for personologists. In briefest form, the theory defines a "nonfitting relation among cognitions" (1957, p. 3) which is termed *cognitive dissonance*. When such a condition exists, the person will attempt to eliminate or reduce the dissonance, that is, "cognitive dissonance is a motivating state of affairs" (1962, p. 3). For example, the cognition (belief) that smoking causes lung cancer would be dissonant with a smoker's awareness of his continued indulgence. The smoker is assumed to be thus motivated to reduce the dissonance, which he can do in a number of different ways: quit smoking, disbelieve the medical reports on smoking and cancer, and so forth.

BASIC DEFINITIONS

In his 1957 book, Festinger was interested in exploring some of the implications of the rather simple notions presented above. He tried to present the theory in as precise a form as possible, of course, but he was not unwilling to retain general suggestive statements where data were insufficient to allow more detailed conceptualization. The resulting theory has often been accused of being too vague, but "enlightened vagueness" is often more virtue than vice. Note the following discussion of a key construct, cognitive "elements"—between which cognitive dissonance may exist.

These elements refer to what has been called cognition, that is, the things a person knows about himself, about his behavior, and about his

125

surroundings. These elements, then, are "knowledges," if I may coin the plural form of the word. Some of these elements represent knowledge about onself: what one does, what one feels, what one wants or desires, what one is, and the like. Other elements of knowledge concern the world in which one lives: what is where, what leads to what, what things are satisfying or painful or inconsequential or important, etc. (1957, p. 9).

The reader of this statement will undoubtedly have a feeling for the way in which Festinger uses the term "cognitive elements," but the lack of precision is often annoying to psychologists, who are very aware of the difficulty of assessing what another person is thinking and feeling. Rather than introduce artificial rigor and precision, Festinger acknowledged the vagueness and stated simply that there are a number of situations in which one can be reasonably certain of the cognitions of another person.

By 1962, however, enough research had been done to indicate some of the difficulties that arise from this vague definition; it was noted that it might be preferable to define a cognitive element as knowledge of an event that "can be shown to influence . . . behavior" (Lawrence and Festinger, 1962, p. 37). In practice, a definition of this type requires the researcher to demonstrate observable criteria for the inferred cognitions and hence is superior in a scientific sense.

Cognitive elements, however defined, may be related to each other in several ways. Two elements may be *irrelevant* to one another ("Today is Saturday" and "Black is the color of my true love's hair"). They may be relevant and *dissonant* (nonfitting) or they may be relevant and *consonant* (fitting). The two elements are in a dissonant relation if, considering these two alone, the opposite of one element would follow from the other: ". . . more formally, *x* and *y* are dissonant if not-*x* follows from *y*" (1957, p. 13, italics deleted). If one element does follow from the other, the two are said to be consonant.

These definitions of relations look more precise and rigorous than the definition of elements, but the appearance is misleading. In particular, the phrase "follow from" is not always easy to understand in a specific situation. Clearly, it does not refer to purely logical consistency, although "Man will reach the moon" is dissonant with "No space ship will be able to leave the earth's atmosphere" on such grounds. More generally, however, "follow from" describes a relation between elements that may have its source in logic, in the culture or subgroup, or in personal experience, just to name a few. "I am eating with my fingers" is dissonant with knowledge about table etiquette in this country; it may not be dissonant in another culture. "I am getting poor grades" may be dissonant for one student, consonant for another. The attempts to specify a reasonable definition of "follow from" remain a continuing endeavor, possibly the most important endeavor for the future of dissonance theory. As the last example indicates, a poor grade (an unpleasant event) may be dissonant for an "A" student but not for a "D" student. Some may say that it must be dissonant even for the "D" student since he certainly desires pleasant experiences (high grades). To say, however, that all unpleasant events produce dissonance would incorporate phenomena for which the theory is clearly not designed. The unpleasant event must be "unexpected," in some realistic or even irrational sense, before dissonance occurs.

Dissonance varies in magnitude. Festinger notes that one obvious determinant of how much dissonance exists is the importance of the elements involved. "I am not studying" will produce more dissonance if you know tomorrow brings a final examination than it will if tomorrow promises only a short quiz. "Importance," in later works, has become associated with degree of motivation; that is, the hungrier you are, the more pain you experience (or in the case of an examination, the more you want to achieve success), the more important the relevant cognitions are likely to be (Lawrence and Festinger, 1962).

Another determinant of dissonance magnitude is the number of elements that are dissonant with another. Obviously, a person holds a great number of beliefs and opinions at any given time. The total amount of dissonance created by a new element would have to be assessed by some kind of summation of the dissonance between it and each of the other cognitions.

DISSONANCE REDUCTION

When dissonance exists, the person is motivated to reduce or eliminate the dissonance. The greater the dissonance, the greater the pressure that exists to reduce it. This motivational paradigm is in the tradition of common physiological drive theories. Dissonance and hunger both lead to attempts at reduction of their respective states.

How dissonance is reduced is a question roughly comparable to the question of how hunger is reduced. It cannot be answered in specific terms apart from the situation the person is facing. However, in general terms, Festinger noted three important means of dissonance reduction: (1) behavior, (2) changing an attitude or belief, and (3) adding new cognitive elements. For example, if dissonance exists between "I do not enjoy getting wet" and "I am standing in the rain," I can eliminate the dissonance by walking inside (behavior). I might, however, change my attitude about getting wet—"I enjoy getting wet"—and stay outside. Finally, I might try to reduce the dissonance by dreaming up new cognitive elements that are consonant with my awareness of my soaking clothes—"My hair needs washing," "Adversity strengthens the soul," or "Lightning is certainly beautiful."

In many cases, adding new cognitive elements requires active search, as with a smoker who combs the medical journals for any report of methodological inadequacies in lung cancer research. Festinger (1957) gives an example of a primitive culture in which people believed that people are always good. This belief conflicted with rather obvious evidence to the contrary. Dissonance was reduced by the addition of a "new" cultural belief: evil ghosts exist and often enter the bodies of "good" people, making them do "bad" things.

Most of the theory has to do with change, changes in behavior and changes in attitudes, in particular. Very often, the reduction of dissonance may occur either through change of behavior or through change of belief, and thus Festinger spent some time discussing features of situations that would predispose a person one way or the other. Such considerations have to do with the determinants of resistance to change.

An element of information about the physical environment, for example, is often difficult to change. One cannot easily believe "It is not raining" when it really is raining. When the information concerns the social environment, the restraints are usually lessened. "People think I'm nice" is a belief that could easily change to "People think I'm rotten," even without an actual change in the social perceptions of others. In other words, the "facts" of physical reality are generally subject to quick and easy validation; they are not ambiguous, and most people hold rigorously similar views about them. The "facts" of the social environment, on the other hand, are ambiguous, not easily verified, and found in significant varieties. The contrast is somewhat like the contrast between a photograph and an inkblot; like the physical environment, what people see in a photograph does not differ much from person to person, but in the inkblot, my "nude on a lopsided elephant" may be your "painted flowers on a broken teacup."

The import of this discussion is to suggest that when information about the physical environment is dissonant with a person's behavior, it is the behavior that is likely to change. When the social environment is involved, the belief or attitude is more susceptible to modification. As we have mentioned, the theory of cognitive dissonance is often considered a theory of attitude change. Although such a label is somewhat misleading, it is appropriate in the sense that the theory's more interesting hypotheses deal with social interaction and the social environment, and, hence, with attitude change.

Changing a cognitive element that is related to one's behavior is, of course, often difficult. The behavior may be irrevocable—murder, for example. It may be involuntary, as a facial "tic." Change may be painful, or it may result in financial loss. The behavior may be satisfying, apart from its dissonant characteristics. Resistance to change in one's behavior does not mean that cognitions about one's behavior cannot change, but rather that heavy pressures exist to make cognition conform to "reality." One could say the same for cognitions about the environment, with the qualification that social "reality" is much less clearly defined than physical "reality." Again, the effect of these statements is to channel most of the theory's predictions into the area of social beliefs and attitudes.

APPLICATIONS

Having said all this, we have progressed little beyond an amplification of our original statement that when two cognitive elements "do not fit" then the person is motivated to reduce or eliminate the dissonance. Festinger's greatest influence stems from his insightful discussions of the implications of his relatively simple theoretical propositions. His 1957 book contained four main sections which have remained the focal point research: (1) the consequences of decisions, (2) forced compliance, (3) voluntary and involuntary exposure to information, and (4) social support. Each of these sections will be discussed in turn, with, however, only brief mention of the last two.

DECISION CONSEQUENCES

Festinger's theory deals with that part of a decision usually ignored by psychological theories: What happens after a decision is made? Dissonance is almost certain to exist from a decision or a choice between two (or more) possibilities. The attractive aspects of the rejected alternative and the unattractive characteristics of the chosen alternative are both dissonant with awareness of the decision. The dissonance can be reduced by *revoking the decision,* but such an action is often impossible, or, if possible, not very beneficial; one source of dissonance would be substituted for another. The dissonance can be reduced by what Festinger calls *"establishing cognitive overlap."* Increased emphasis on (or arbitrary creation of) similarities between the two alternatives has the effect of denying the decision. "They're both the same, so it really didn't matter which I chose." Festinger gives the example of a man choosing between a dinner party and a concert. After deciding in favor of the dinner, he recalls that the host has a fine record collection. He hasn't given up music after all!

A third and more widely studied way to reduce postdecision dissonance is *to change one's attitude toward the alternatives.* The chosen possibility is seen as more attractive, the rejected alternative as less so.

The grapes passed by were sour, and the lemons you got were unusually sweet.

A typical experiment (Jecker, 1964) had high school girls rate the attractiveness of a dozen popular records. Two records that had been rated as moderately attractive were then offered as gifts. After choosing one, each girl then rated all of the records again. Scores composed of adding the increase in attractiveness of the chosen record and the decrease in attractiveness of the not-chosen record indicated a substantial dissonance reduction as compared with a control condition in which each girl received both records.

FORCED COMPLIANCE

A second area of application is in situations where a person is for some reason forced to behave in a way he would ordinarily not.

He is forced in the sense of being offered a reward for behaving in a certain way, for example, or of being threatened with punishment. A person might be given money (bribed) for lying on the witness stand; another might say he thinks X is innocent because he fears he will be killed for stating his true opinion. Because much of the research in forced compliance deals with situations of this type, in which a person publicly says something counter to his true opinion or belief, the research is often referred to as *counter-attitudinal.*

The knowledge of what one really believes, in such a case, is dissonant with the knowledge that one is acting or speaking in a way counter to this belief. The prediction is that the dissonance reduction will usually take the form of an attitude change so that the belief is more in line with the behavior. A perjuring witness will begin to believe his lies or at least consider them less of a fabrication than he did before he spoke them. The intriguing aspect of such situations is the relationship between the amount of reward or punishment for compliance and the amount of dissonance. If the reward or punishment is just sufficient to gain compliance, dissonance is created. However, as the degree of punishment or reward increases beyond the minimum necessary, the amount of dissonance decreases. Knowledge of a high reward or of great punishment, in other words, is another cognitive element; such knowledge is consonant with the knowledge of alien behavior, hence dissonance is reduced. For example, to publicly state that you do not believe in obeying laws would be very dissonant if you did it for $1, but for $1,000,000 . . . ?

We have introduced, in this discussion, another important theoretical construct, that of *justification.* Formally stated, dissonance theory asserts that the more justification there is for an alien act, the less dissonance exists. Suppose the justification is slight, as in the case in which you pocket a mere $1 for advocating something against your principles.

Festinger suggests that pressure is produced by dissonance to change your private belief so that it corresponds to your public statement—that is, you will not think so highly of "law-abidingness" as you did before. Phrased slightly differently, the *less* money I pay you to express an opinion you do not hold, the *more* likely you are to change your opinion. This is just one of the nonobvious predictions from dissonance theory that have excited psychologists in all fields.

In a now classic experiment on these hypotheses, Festinger and Carlsmith (1959) had subjects work for an hour on a boring task. When the subjects had finished, they were asked to "lie" to the next incoming subject and tell him the experiment was really interesting and fun. For this falsehood, they were offered either $1 or $20. In a later rating of interest in the boring task, those with small justification ($1) saw it as significantly more interesting than those who were paid $20. To say it was enjoyable when it was boring was assumed to be dissonant; if the justification (money received) was insufficient to "warrant" this falsehood, the dissonance pressured the person into believing the experiment was really interesting after all.

Aronson and Carlsmith (1963) tested the same hypothesis by using punishment instead of reward. Children were told not to play with an attractive toy while the experimenter was gone from the room, under mild threat ("I will be annoyed") or severe threat ("I will be very angry and take away all the toys"). Toys in the mild threat condition decreased in attractiveness, a significant difference when compared with toys in the severe threat condition. In theory, the dissonance between wanting to play with the toys and not doing so is resolved either by a change in attitude (decreased attractiveness) or by high justification (severe threat).

VOLUNTARY AND INVOLUNTARY EXPOSURE TO INFORMATION

Voluntary seeking of information, according to the theory, is an attempt to add cognitive elements that will reduce dissonance, as with a man who has just decided to buy car A rather than car B. Generally, he should seek information favorable to A and possibly unfavorable to B. If by chance he is involuntarily exposed to the opposite kinds of material—favorable to B or unfavorable to A—he might well react defensively, with tactics designed to invalidate the information. "It's just an advertisement for B, all a bunch of baloney." The evidence in support of these hypotheses is not easily summarized; the reader is referred to an excellent review by Freedman and Sears (1965).

SOCIAL SUPPORT

"Social support" includes a body of theory and research that belongs more in the area of social psychology than in personality; it, also, will be passed over much too quickly, with only the slightest indication of the phenomena under study. Suppose you believe in God and that person X does not. Festinger has suggested that this state of affairs is dissonant, primarily because of the peculiar role other people play in defining social "reality," the world of opinions, attitudes, and beliefs. Your belief in God requires social support in the form of other people with the same belief. If this social support is not forthcoming, dissonance is created in almost the same manner as when a "knowledge" about the physical environment is not verified by physical reality. Reducing dissonance caused by lack of social support may be achieved by changing your belief or opinion, trying to change that of the other person, or reducing the importance of the other person by categorizing: "He's uneducated, misguided," and the like. This list, like most of Festinger's lists, is not meant to be exhaustive of all possibilities but merely to cite some common examples.

THEORY MODIFICATIONS

The theory of cognitive dissonance was originally formulated in a way that would allow for maximum clarification and modification if experimental evidence and subsequent conceptualization warranted. Since Festinger's 1957 book, at least two significant attempts at theory modification have been published. One, by Brehm and Cohen (1962), utilized available empirical evidence as the basis for suggesting theory revision in two main aspects. Both aspects refer to characteristics of decision situations to which dissonance theory can be most effectively applied. One such characteristic is *volition*, which means that the more the decision is perceived to have been made "freely," the more the dissonance. A person who "had no choice" need feel no dissonance. In practice, the volition construct does not abrogate the relevance of forced compliance studies because the subjects are "forced" only in the sense of being offered rewards or threatened. They do not *have* to comply, they can *always* choose not to. Volition is therefore involved and dissonance predictions apply.

The second characteristic of dissonant decision situations is *commitment*. When a person has made his choice, he has made his commitment. Until that moment of truth, however, dissonance predictions do not apply. Brehm and Cohen are reemphasizing the role of dissonance theory as one pertaining to the consequences of decisions and not to decision-making itself; dissonance theory is a *postdecisional* theory. In addition, commitment implies that changing the decision itself is unlikely. Brehm and Cohen see these situations as the ones in which the "spectacular" predictions of dissonance theory occur, predictions contrary to those made by other theories. For example, in the Jecker experiment on the choice of popular records described above, the dissonance effect occurred when the girls chose one or the other of the two records offered. In another condition, the girls were led to believe their choice might not be binding, that there was a slight possibility of receiving both records. With this uncertainty present, the girls did not change their attractiveness ratings differently from the control group. Their decision, in other words, was not final; commitment had not occurred.

The second major attempt at theory modification was a fascinating attempt to apply dissonance theory to "nonverbal organisms," a euphemism for rats. Apart from the highly unusual claim that a theory about human cognitions can illuminate certain stubborn problems in understanding rat learning, the Lawrence and Festinger (1962) treatise is of importance in that its work with "nonverbal organisms" forces clarification of basic constructs.

The specific problem areas discussed were partial reward, delay of reward, and increased effort expenditure. All three tend to *decrease* "learning" by most indicators, but all three result in increased resistance to extinction, an indication of *increased* learning. The notable similarity among the three is that they are all "something the animal will avoid if given an opportunity to do so" (Lawrence and Festinger, 1962, p. 31). The animal will choose 100% reward over 50% (partial) reward, no delay over delay of reward, and no effort over effort. All three, in other words, are *deterrents* to action, where a deterrent is defined as ". . . any variable which, when increased in magnitude, makes for decreased willingness to perform an action . . ." (Lawrence and Festinger, 1962, p. 39).

The reader will perhaps anticipate the dissonance interpretation of such situations: The awareness of the unpleasantness of the act and the knowledge that he has performed is dissonant for the rat. He is motivated to reduce the dissonance. How does a rat reduce dissonance?

How does a human reduce dissonance in similar situations? Aronson and Mills (1959) had female subjects volunteer for participation in group discussions on the psychology of sex. Before joining the group, however, the girls were required to undergo mild or severe embarrassment (deterrence)—a kind of initiation ceremony. In the "severe" group, subjects read out loud descriptions of sexual behavior and obscene words in the presence of a male experimenter; the "mild" subjects read some mild sexual material. Then both groups listened to a tape-recorded discussion, described as rather dull and purported to be a sample of the discussion group's activities. The girls who had experienced the severe initiation rated the group more favorably than those who had experienced the mild initiation. According to the theory, those with severe deterrents to joining the group had to rate the group favorably in order to reduce their dissonance between knowledge of the deterrent and awareness of joining. "Why would I have gone through all that if the group weren't really interesting?"

Our rats were faced with a similar dilemma. They have performed in spite of a deterrence. They cannot be asked to rate their interest on a 7-point scale, of course, but they can be asked the same type of question in a different way: "If we stop all extrinsic reward, how long will you continue performing?" Assuming that more interest equals more persistence, the rats will rate the task higher by taking more trials to extinguish.

It is not our task to consider the problems of animal learning nor to evaluate the dissonance contribution to such issues. The clarification of definitions required by animal research, however, marks an extension of Festinger's theory with important implications for human experimentation. For example, dissonance is induced when one performs in a situation with deterrence to such performance, where deterrence is defined as above.

In discussing the process by which rats come to "like" unpleasant activities, Lawrence and Festinger (1962) suggest that "subordinate" animal drives such as exploration, manipulation, and sensory stimulation are brought into play. To reduce dissonance in the face of deterrents, the rat may begin "to note and pay attention to aspects of the situation that satisfy these other motivations, ... discovering new items of information about the consequences of its actions that are consonant with it. Loosely speaking, we can say that the animal has discovered 'extra attractions' in the situation" (Lawrence and Festinger, 1962, p. 47). Human studies rarely discuss in such detail the mechanism by which unpleasant situations come to be "liked," that is, rated as more interesting and attractive. The result of this is a mysterious air about much dissonance experimentation; the mind is "playing tricks" of some highly unusual type. If the more detailed descriptions of processes were executed on the human level, much of the mystery would surely disappear.

A tremendous amount of research has been generated by the cognitive dissonance theory. Often a study will merely confirm or cast suspicion on some hypothesis, but often conceptualization is improved and new major concepts emerge. An example of the latter case is an experiment by Freedman (1963), who varied both the time at which justification was given and the amount of justification. He had subjects write a series of random numbers. High justification instructions explained the usefulness of people's implicit notions of "randomness"; low justification instructions stated the data would be of no use, but since the subjects had been scheduled for the task they should go ahead anyway. These instructions were given either before or after the task. Results showed that ratings of task enjoyment were greater with lower justification (a dissonance theory prediction) only if justification preceded the task. If justification followed the task, enjoyment was greater in the high justification condition.

Freedman asserted that the *time of justification* was important and that dissonance theory applied only when the justification came before the task. If the justification followed the behavior, he argued, it serves as a reinforcement. The typical reinforcement theory predictions were confirmed: the higher the reward (justification), the higher the enjoyment.

Freedman's research is a good example of the never-ending process of theory extension through research. Insko (1967) has written a good review and commentary on research in this area, with all the minor variations and conceptual suggestions that will someday be incorporated into another major theory revision.

SUMMARY

Festinger defined a nonfitting relation between cognitive elements as dissonance and hypothesized that such a state motivated the person to reduce the dissonance. From these simple beginnings sprung an enormous amount of exciting research. The puzzle remains: Although theories based on inconsistency and drives toward consistency are ubiquitous, the theory of cognitive dissonance clearly represents some kind of shift in conceptualization and in research directions. The shift has had a momentous effect on all of psychology. What was the shift? It is not easy to identify. The focus on what happens *after* a decision, rather than before, illuminated a hitherto obscure area of psychology. The emphasis on cognitions without the typical loss of behavior-relevance was a notable achievement. The ingenuity of Festinger and his co-workers in perceiving the areas in which a theory of consistency could be applied was a factor. But when all is said and done, the puzzle remains: What was the shift, why was it made, and why was it so important?

Whatever the answer, the theory of cognitive dissonance has made its contribution and will continue to do so. The four main areas of research: decision consequences, forced compliance, exposure to information, and social support. The major constructs supplementing the basic theory: amount and time of justification, volition, commitment, and the like. In terms of the amount of research reported in current issues of major academic journals, probably no other theory in this book exceeds Festinger's cognitive dissonance theory. Whether right or wrong as a theory, this is one of the most significant achievements any theory can obtain.

REFERENCES

Aronson, E., & Carlsmith, J. The effect of severity of threat on the devalua-ation of forbidden behavior. *Journal of Abnormal Social Psychology*, 1963, **66**, 584–588.

Aronson, E., & Mills, J. The effect of severity of initiation on liking for a group. *Journal of Abnormal Social Psychology*, 1959, **59**, 177–181.

Brehm, J., & Cohen, A. *Explorations in cognitive dissonance*. New York: Wiley, 1962.

Festinger, L. *A theory of cognitive dissonance*. Stanford, Calif.: Stanford Univ. Press, 1957.

Festinger, L. Cognitive dissonance. *Scientific American*, October, 1962.

Festinger, L. (Ed.) *Conflict, decision, and dissonance*. Stanford, Calif.: Stanford Univ. Press, 1964.

Festinger, L., & Carlsmith, J. Cognitive consequences of forced compliance. *Journal of Abnormal and Social Psychology*, 1959, **58**, 203–210.

Freedman, J. Attitudinal effects of insufficient justification. *Journal of Personality*, 1963, **31**, 371–385.

Freedman, J., & Sears, D. Selective exposure. In L. Berkowitz (Ed.), *Advances in experimental social psychology*. Vol. II. New York: Academic Press, 1965.

Insko, C. A. *Theories of attitude change*. New York: Appleton-Century-Crofts, 1967.

Jecker, J. The cognitive effects of conflict and dissonance. In L. Festinger (Ed.), *Conflict, decision, and dissonance*. Stanford, Calif.: Stanford Univ. Press, 1964.

Lawrence, D. H., & Festinger, L. *Deterrents and reinforcement: The psychology of insufficient reward*. Stanford, Calif.: Stanford Univ. Press, 1962.

14

The theories in this book represent a case history of an academic discipline. Human behavior is a constant across all of them; it is the thing to be explained, although the attempts to explain it differ in many respects. This chapter provides a brief overall summary of these approaches and also looks at some of the trends, newer developments, and theories not included in this book but likely to appear in similar books in years to come.

A theory of personality is a set of constructs deemed necessary for the explanation of most important human behavior. (Table 3 summarizes the theories in this book in terms of important contributions and major theoretical concepts.) The most ubiquitous kind of construct is one that represents an intrapersonal urge; examples of this kind are need, drive, motive, and certain kinds of traits (dynamic). Also common are constructs dealing with structure—for example, habits, expectancies, regions in a "life space," and certain kinds of traits. Structural constructs refer to relatively enduring, usually learned characteristics of the person which function primarily to direct rather than to motivate behavior. A third common type of construct refers to characteristics of the environment that have "pulling" power, or, in theoretical terms, valence or incentive. All theories have something to say about the three areas covered by these three construct-types, although the same construct may cover all three (as with some trait approaches) and various theories differ in their emphasis on one or the other. Historically, personality theory had its beginnings in the emphasis on the "inner urge" or push constructs. Early Freudian theorists spent much time examining such determinants of behavior, and the so-called motivational emphasis of Allport, Murray, and Murphy represents conceptual systems continuing that tradition. When experimental learning theory began making great scientific strides in the middle twentieth century, structural concepts such as habit began increasing in prominence in personality theory as well. Miller and Dollard's theory is the most direct representative of such change, but even Cattell, a trait theorist like Allport, has a much more pronounced structural emphasis than his predecessor.

There has always been a recognized need for the third type of construct, some means by which a theorist can incorporate the situation

Table 3

Outline of Personality Theories

CHAPTER	MAJOR CONSTRUCTS	INFLUENTIAL CONTRIBUTIONS
2 Allport	Trait. Functional autonomy.	Trait approach. Individualism. Nonhistorical analysis of behavior.
3 Murphy	Canalization. Autism.	Eclecticism. Influence of needs on perception. Field theory approach.
4 Murray	Needs, press, and thema. Proceedings.	Longitudinal study of human behavior. "Need" approach. Thematic Apperception Test (TAT).
5 Sheldon	Endomorphy and viscerotonia. Mesomorphy and somatotonia. Ectomorphy and cerebrotonia.	Relation of personality to biological or constitutional attributes.
6 Cattell	Source traits. Ergs, engrams. Dynamic subsidiation, dynamic lattice.	Trait approach. Factor analysis. Test development.
7 Miller and Dollard	Cue-producing response (thought). Imitation. Approach-avoidance gradients (conflicts). Frustration-aggression.	Learning approach. Rigorous research methods.
8 Bandura and Walters	Modeling. Self-control.	Social learning approach. Behavior modification techniques.
9 Rogers	Need for self-actualization. Need for positive self-regard. Empathy, congruence, and unconditional positive regard.	"Humanism" (client-centered approach).
10 Lewin	Vector. Valence. Life space.	Introduction of social variables into intrapersonal theory. Field theory. Ahistorical emphasis. Intrapersonal conflict. Uncompleted tasks. Level of aspiration.
11 Kelly	Personal constructs.	Redefinition of "traits" as conceptual categories.

Table 3 (continued)

Outline of Personality Theories

CHAPTER	MAJOR CONSTRUCTS	INFLUENTIAL CONTRIBUTIONS
12 Atkinson	Achievement motivation. Motive, expectancy, and incentive.	Development of TAT scoring methods. Extensive study of achievement.
13 Festinger	Cognitive dissonance.	Attitude change research. Postdecisional emphasis. Social emphasis.

or environment into his predictions, but such rumblings were rarely translated into effective theoretical activity. Murray's "press" was an early attempt. Lewin made one of the most significant breaks with tradition and he did so in two respects. First, he developed the concept of valence, which combines the perceived environment and the varying attractiveness of its parts. Second, he defined valence in such a way that both intrapersonal urges (needs) and extrapersonal characteristics (situation) fed into it. Atkinson's "incentive" construct continued in this tradition. Kelly's theory of personal constructs, on the other hand, brought in situational determinants through another door. With Kelly's emphasis on how the person "construes" his environment, the study of situation became more prominent than the study of needs.

In Festinger's theory of cognitive dissonance, "situation" entered the equations almost by default. While dissonance theory applies to all beliefs, those dealing with social situations generally are the only cognitions satisfying the conditions under which dissonance predictions become interesting. Beliefs about the physical environment are subject to rigorous testing, but beliefs about the social environment are difficult to test and some are even self-validating. The theory therefore becomes channeled almost entirely into the area of social attitudes and, hence, into the social environment.

The move toward constructs dealing with the environment will certainly continue. A similar trend in personality theories has already been mentioned: an increasing emphasis on interpersonal or social behavior. It is true of Festinger's theory, for example, and the trend is also clearly visible in Bandura and Walter's theory, especially when it is compared with the older Miller-Dollard approach. There is an increasing reluctance to accept data from animal experimentation and from nonsocial human studies. This reluctance is no doubt a function of the burgeoning research on social interaction and of the amazing sophistication in experimental design developed under the auspices of such theorists as Festinger and Bandura. The findings of experimental social psychologists and sociologists are also now feeding into personology.

Another trend in personality theories is a sharpening focus upon cognitive constructs. Even in Freudian theory, there has been a gradual shift in study from the "id" (motivational processes) to the "ego" (reality processes). Perception, attention, and cognition have become much more prominent in personological discussions. Festinger's and Kelly's theories have this emphasis in a high degree, but almost all the theories in this book have changed over a period of time to a more cognitive position.

These trends toward situational constructs and toward social and cognitive emphases, of course, are by no means unrelated. The important *situational* determinants of human behavior are largely *social,* and the person's beliefs, attitudes, and *cognitions* about this social situation are the more proximal determinants.

The kind of constructs to be employed in the understanding of human personality has always been a topic for vigorous debate in personality, as it should be. Apart from the trends noted above, much recent discussion has centered on the nature of personality "traits," which have long been an important construct. Kelly, as we noted, redefined traits as conceptual categories instead of attributes and began studying the perceiver instead of the object of reference. Mischel (1968) provided an excellently argued and thoroughly documented case against the wisdom of using a trait approach in theory or in assessment procedures. He also presented an alternative, very behavioral approach with a focus on controlling conditions. Similar to Bandura and Walters', Mischel's theory holds great promise and, given a few years for reaction and evaluation by the scientific community, will probably become a major force in the field.

While Mischel attacks traits, others are busy in attempts to salvage the potential from the constructs that have, admittedly, been basic to personology for all these years. Thoroughly cognizant of the wealth of disparaging data and conceptual difficulties, Norman and his associates have produced a series of highly sophisticated studies on the nature of traits. Norman has found, for example, strong empirical evidence to support the view that traits are culturally determined conceptual schemes and that they may have more relevance for the "rater" than for the "ratee" (Passini and Norman, 1966). Beyond this, however, Norman has also begun developing statistical techniques for analyzing the *separate* effects of rater concepts and ratee attributes upon trait ratings (Norman and Goldberg, 1966). In other words, he is advancing the view that traits as typically assessed are an amalgam of concepts and attributes and that any "extremist" view is at least premature. More than this, however, Norman's extremely rigorous research is adding some light to a debate characterized by an abundance of heat.

Looking at other potential influences on the field, it appears likely that learning theory will again influence personology, as it has through Hull and Skinner in the past. More physiological theories, Hebb's being one very important example, have improved the conceptualization of "general operator" constructs such as "arousal." The constructs are called "general operators" because, more or less, they function in a general way to affect whatever specific thoughts or behaviors are ongoing at the moment. Blum (1961), for example, has incorporated such constructs into a model of the mind, which is designed to aid research on the general functioning of human mental processes. Blum has also been a pioneer in the use of hypnosis as a research instrument. The use of hypnosis, together with generally small sample studies made necessary by the long training procedures and careful attention to experimental controls, has frightened many psychologists, but the validity problems of hypnotic techniques and small samples are neither uncommon nor insurmountable. The future will probably be more excited about Blum's approach than the present is.

As cognitive processes become more important, computers will undoubtedly increase in importance as vehicles for personality theories. Loehlin (1968) has published a book on computer models of personality, which now suffer mostly from the lack of suitable models to "plug in." More promising, perhaps, is the use of computers as complex and interdependent "confederates" in interaction with humans to study human behavior in controlled but realistic social interaction (see also Messick, 1967).

Finally, the continually recognized need for integration of data from different levels of analysis will certainly come to more effective actualization. Results from biology, psychology, sociology, and anthropology, as well as from economics and political science, all apply to human behavior. Notable attempts at integration have begun (Parsons and Shils, 1953; Yinger, 1965) and will continue.

One major development has been slighted in this book and in this chapter: a tremendous surge in "humanistic" personality theories and essays. Among the theories in this book, Rogers' is the most representative of this approach. Maslow's *Toward a Psychology of Being* (1962) is also basic. With the exception of Rogers', these approaches have not produced much research, and what has been done is generally of poor quality. Recently the most notable development in this area has been the extension of such approaches to group "psychotherapy" with "normal" individuals: various groups with slightly different functions have been labeled sensitivity training groups (T groups), encounter groups, marathon encounter groups, nude marathon encounter groups, and so on. The philosophy and activity of such groups are centered around the ideas that man strives to better himself (self-actualization) and that man has the abilities to do so if the situation is right. The situation is presumably right when interchange is characterized by freedom of thought and action, honesty, openness, human warmth and support, and so forth. An encounter group, for example, typically begins with the specification of group norms: you are to be concerned with the open and honest expression of your feelings in the "here and now." Often social norms operative in the society are reversed: hostile remarks are not to be inhibited, touching is encouraged.

I must admit to being alternatively excited and infuriated by these new developments. And I must confess that I do not fully understand what they represent in the history of personology. But I have an opinion. Usually in the history of any discipline, when some critical factors are being overlooked, someone calls attention to this fact. The reason critical factors are overlooked, however, is usually that there is no easy or productive way to handle them scientifically, either in theory or in research. The attention-calling, therefore, takes on an almost religious flavor, often with anti-intellectual and anti-scientific aspects—which makes it infuriating to the scientist, of course. Gradually, the concepts become refined, new methods are developed, and the critical factors are incorporated into classic scientific systems. What are the critical factors in the "humanistic" psychologies? If one could answer this question properly, there wouldn't be humanistic psychologies. There are factors in the areas of ethics, "higher" motivations, and the role of social norms and rules in human behavior, to mention a few. Greater specification will come, but not for a time.

So we have come to the end of our story. Like all "ends," it is more a "commencement." The history of personology as a science is very short, and we have reviewed only the beginnings.

REFERENCES

Blum, G. S. A model of the mind. New York: Wiley, 1961.

Loehlin, J. C. Computer models of personality. New York: Random House, 1968.

Maslow, A. H. Toward a psychology of being. Princeton, N. J.: Van Nostrand, 1962.

Messick, D. M. Interdependent decision strategies in zero-sum games: A computer-controlled study. Behavioral Science, 1967, 12, 33–48.

Mischel, W. *Personality and assessment.* New York: Wiley, 1968.

Norman, W. T., & Goldberg, L. R. Raters, ratees, and randomness in personality structure. *Journal of Personality and Social Psychology,* 1966, **4,** 681–691.

Parsons, T., & Shils, E. A. *Toward a general theory of action.* Cambridge, Mass.: Harvard Univ. Press, 1953.

Passini, F. T., & Norman, W. T. A universal conception of personality structure? *Journal of Personality and Social Psychology,* 1966, **4,** 44–49.

Yinger, J. M. *Toward a field theory of behavior.* New York: McGraw-Hill, 1965.

NAME INDEX

Allport, G. W., 5–18, 28, 47, 49, 51, 137, 138
Alpert, R., 112, 118, 119
Armitage, S. G., 78
Aronfreed, J., 76
Aronson, E., 131, 133
Atkinson, J. W., 4, 9, 28, 99, 111–124, 139
Bandura, A., 66–83, 138, 139, 140
Bertocci, P. A., 12
Bieri, J., 109
Birch, D., 10, 121, 122
Birney, R. C., 119
Blum, G. S., 4, 141
Bonarius, J. C. J., 109
Brehm, J. W., 132
Brown, J. S., 58f.
Carlsmith, J. M., 131
Cattell, R. B., 4, 46–52, 137, 138
Chein, I., 25, 26
Clark, R. A., 111, 113
Cohen, A. R., 132
Cowen, J. E., 118
Cronbach, L. J., 2
Deutsch, M., 91, 98, 100
Dollard, J., 53–65, 66, 67, 68, 70, 96, 137, 138, 139
Doob, L. W., 61
Dreger, R. M., 88
Escalona, S., 99, 114
Eysenck, H. J., 4
Farquhar, W. W., 119
Feather, N. T., 113, 118, 122
Festinger, L., 4, 13, 25, 94, 99, 111, 114, 125–136, 139, 140
Freedman, J., 131, 134f.
Freud, S., 4, 53, 137, 140
Freund, K., 79
Goldberg, L. R., 140
Grusec, J. E., 78
Haber, R. N., 112, 118, 119

Hall, C. S., 13, 43
Harris, M. B., 72
Hebb, D. O., 141
Herzberg, A., 77
Holt, R. R., 10
Horner, M., 117
Hovland, C. I., 62
Hull, C. L., 141
Insko, C. A., 135
Jecker, J., 130
Jensen, F., 19
Kagan, J., 119
Karsten, A., 93
Kelly, G. A., 102–110, 138, 139, 140
King, G. F., 78
Kluckhohn, C., 31, 36
Krumboltz, J. D., 119
Kupers, C. J., 76
Lawrence, D. H., 126, 127, 133, 134
Lecky, P., 13
Levine, R., 25, 26
Lewin, K., 27, 28, 39, 53, 58, 91–101, 113, 114, 138, 139
Lindzey, G., 13, 43
Litwin, G. H., 119f.
Loehlin, J. C., 141
Lovaas, O. I., 79
Lowell, E. L., 111, 112, 119
Mahone, C. H., 117
Mandler, G., 118
Maslow, A. H., 3, 90, 141
McClelland, D. C., 111, 112, 113, 119, 121
McDonald, F. J., 70, 72
Meehl, P. E., 2
Menlove, F. L., 78
Messick, D. M., 141
Miller, N. E., 53–65, 66, 67, 68, 70, 96, 137, 138, 139
Mills, J., 133
Mischel, W., 51, 65, 102, 119, 140

144

SUBJECT INDEX

BASIC CONCEPTS IN PSYCHOLOGY SERIES

Edward L. Walker, Editor

GENERAL

PSYCHOLOGY AS A NATURAL AND SOCIAL SCIENCE	Edward L. Walker
TEACHING THE BEGINNING COURSE IN PSYCHOLOGY	Edward L. Walker and Wilbert J. McKeachie
A LABORATORY MANUAL FOR THE CONTROL AND ANALYSIS OF BEHAVIOR	Harlan L. Lane and Daryl J. Bem
QUANTIFICATION IN PSYCHOLOGY	William L. Hays
BASIC STATISTICS	William L. Hays

PSYCHOLOGY: A NATURAL SCIENCE

NEUROPSYCHOLOGY: THE STUDY OF BRAIN AND BEHAVIOR	Charles M. Butter
SENSORY PROCESSES	Mathew Alpern, Merle Lawrence, and David Wolsk
PERCEPTION	Daniel J. Weintraub and Edward L. Walker
HUMAN PERFORMANCE	Paul M. Fitts and Michael I. Posner
CONDITIONING AND INSTRUMENTAL LEARNING	Edward L. Walker

PSYCHOLOGY: A SOCIAL SCIENCE

MOTIVATION: A STUDY OF ACTION	David Birch and Joseph Veroff
THE CONCEPT OF HUMAN DEVELOPMENT	Elton B. McNeil
PSYCHODYNAMICS: THE SCIENCE OF UNCONSCIOUS MENTAL FORCES	Gerald S. Blum
ASSESSMENT OF HUMAN CHARACTERISTICS	E. Lowell Kelly
COGNITIVE PROCESSES	Melvin Manis
SOCIAL PSYCHOLOGY: AN EXPERIMENTAL APPROACH	Robert B. Zajonc
NON-FREUDIAN PERSONALITY THEORIES	P. James Geiwitz
BELIEFS, ATTITUDES, AND HUMAN AFFAIRS	Daryl J. Bem
CLINICAL PSYCHOLOGY: AN EMPIRICAL APPROACH	Erasmus L. Hoch
ABNORMAL PSYCHOLOGY	James Neal Butcher

BROOKS/COLE PUBLISHING COMPANY
A Division of Wadsworth Publishing Company, Inc., Belmont, California

51 B 9965